PYTHON PROGRAMMING

2 book in 1:

Python programming for beginners

Python programming for intermediate

A complete guide from beginner to intermediate on python machine learning, data science, tools

Will Norton

Legal & Disclaimer

The information contained in this book and its contents is not designed to replace or take the place of any form of medical or professional advice; and is not meant to replace the need for independent medical, financial, legal or other professional advice or services, as may be required. The content and information in this book has been provided for educational and entertainment purposes only.

The content and information contained in this book has been compiled from sources deemed reliable, and it is accurate to the best of the Author's knowledge, information and belief. However, the Author cannot guarantee its accuracy and validity and cannot be held liable for any errors and/or omissions. Further, changes are periodically made to this book as and when needed. Where appropriate and/or necessary, you must consult a professional (including but not limited to your doctor, attorney, financial advisor or such other professional advisor) before using any of the suggested remedies, techniques, or information in this book.

Upon using the contents and information contained in this book, you agree to hold harmless the Author from and against any damages, costs, and expenses, including any legal fees potentially resulting from the application of any of the information provided by this book. This disclaimer applies to any loss, damages or injury caused by the use and application, whether directly or indirectly, of any advice or information presented, whether for breach of contract, tort, negligence, personal injury, criminal intent, or under any other cause of action.

You agree to accept all risks of using the information presented inside this book.

You agree that by continuing to read this book, where appropriate and/or necessary, you shall consult a professional (including but not limited to your doctor, attorney, or financial advisor or such other advisor as needed) before using any of the suggested remedies, techniques, or information in this book.

Table of Contents

PYTHON PROGRAMMING

A complete beginners guide
on python machine learning,
data science and tools

Will Norton

Introduction

Python is a programming language that is often recommended for beginners to try messing up things and falling in love with programming. One of the major reasons for the widespread popularity of Python is its simplicity and the power of making things done with less code. Even after the entrance of tens of programming languages in the past decade python doesn't lose its charm and we are pretty confident that is going to stay.

This book is a classical and a layman's introduction to python programming concepts in simple and concise explanations. All the concepts are included with programs so that the reader can understand the essence of the topic.

What is Python?

Python is a programming language that is pretty famous and has a very generous community that produces high-quality projects for various branches of computer science such as Data mining, Machine learning, and Deep learning on a regular basis. It is an old programming language but still solves modern problems perfectly.

This book is not a reference but a smart introduction to python in an easy way. We tried to explain all the concepts in an easy language so that the readers can penetrate the programming concepts in their minds and use them to create some pretty innovative projects.

How to get the most out of this book?

Programming concepts are always understood only if you can practically use them on your own. For this exact reason, we have bundled this book with a lot of programming code examples that will initiate you to code on your own. Already experienced programmers can also use this book as good reference material on python.

There are a lot of books that cover Python in the market but you have chosen us to immerse you into the world of Python programming. We are sure that you will get a good learning experience while reading this book. Let us go!

Chapter 1: What is Python?

This chapter is a comprehensive introduction to python basics and its abilities. We will start with a little history and will then dive into other complex topics. We advise you to use this book both as a reference and learning material.

Python is an explanatory, object-oriented and high-level programming language with dynamic semantics. It can be used as a real cross-platform (running on Linux, macOS, and Windows) language, and its forced indentation syntax makes its code simple and easy to read.

Applications of Python

Python is easier to use than other programming languages. Because Python has a large number of third-party libraries, it is more efficient and faster to use Python to develop application projects. Python is widely used in system management. Multi-national Companies like Industrial Light & Magic use Python to produce special effects in high-budget movies.

Yahoo! is using it (including other technologies) to manage discussion groups. Google uses it to implement many components in web crawlers and search engines. Python is also used in various fields such as computer games and biological information. With the rapid development of artificial intelligence, Python's application has been better popularized.

Python History

Python was founded by Guido van Rossum of the Netherlands. During Thanksgiving Day in 1989, Guido decided to develop a new script interpreter as an inheritance of the ABC language to kill the boredom of Christmas. Python was chosen as the name of the language because he is a fan of BBC TV series "Monty Python's Flying Circus". He wanted to create a mystique about the programming language. For this reason, he named it Python.

Python was born in 1989, but the first public release was issued in 1991, Python2.0 was officially released in October 2000, Python3.0 was officially released in December 2008, and the latest version is Python3.6.5 as of this book is written.

Python is an object-oriented and literal translation computer programming language, as well as a powerful general programming language. It contains a set of perfect and easy-to-understand standard libraries and is supported by a large number of third-party libraries, which can easily accomplish many common tasks.

Its syntax is very simple and clear, unlike most other computer programming languages, it uses a forced indentation to define statement blocks.

Python's Design Style

Python insists on a clear and uniform design style, which makes Python an easy-to-read and easy-to-maintain language that is popular with a large number of users and has a wide range of uses. The general guiding ideology of designers in development is that it is best as long as there is the best way to solve a specific problem.

Python's design philosophy is being elegant, clear, simple and readable.

Python's Object-Oriented philosophy

Python is a programming language that supports object-oriented programming paradigm process. It has a lot of technical abilities that help it to be a better programming language than of procedural languages that are available.

Python developer's philosophy is to use one method, preferably only one method, to do one thing. This is different from most other programming languages. When you are faced with many choices in writing programs in Python, Python developers will usually reject those fancy methods and choose clear, little or no ambiguous syntax. These criteria are what we usually call Python's maxim.

You can see a famous article written by Tim Peters on python basics. It introduces some important principles that need to be paid attention to when writing beautiful Python programs, to understand Python's design philosophy. Also, you can refer to relevant websites to learn about Python's design philosophy.

In the next section, we will discuss installing third-party libraries in Python language. This is a basic skill that is necessary for python programmers to learn before dealing with hard coding skills. It is pretty basic and very useful for beginners. Let us learn about it in detail.

How to install the third-party libraries?

Python has a powerful standard library, and the Python community provides a large number of third-party libraries in a similar way to the standard library. If strong standard libraries have laid for the foundation for Python's development, third party libraries are responsible for Python's continuous development. With continuous updates of Python, some stable third-party libraries have been added to the standard library.

When Anaconda was installed, Python's standard libraries and some commonly used third-party libraries were installed with a Python interpreter. You can enter "pip list" at the Windows prompt to view the installed libraries. All the installed libraries will then appear on the output screen.

If you want to use a third-party library that is not installed, you must install it using the installation method described below. Beginners can skip this now if it is too overwhelming to concentrate on. You can always come back to this section for understanding the installation of third-party modules.

1) Source installation

Many third-party libraries are open source, almost all of which can be found on GitHub or PyPI. Most of the source codes found are available in zip, tar.zip, tar.bz2 format compression packages. After unpacking these compressed packages, you will usually see a setup.py file. Open the Windows command line window and enter the folder.

Run the following command to install:

run setup.py // This is the usually used command

2) Package Manager

Many programming languages now have package managers, such as Ruby's gem and nodejs's npm. Python is certainly no exception. Pip and conda can be used to install third-party libraries.

(1) pip Management of Python Library.

You should remember that when Python installation was introduced earlier, one of the options that it offers was to install the pip Package Manager. Of course, if Anaconda is selected for installation it should be noted that the package manager has already installed it automatically. If the pip package manager has been installed, enter pip on the command line and click enter, and you can see the results.

pip {Enter the third-party name}

When installing a third-party library using the pip installation module, the system will automatically download the installation file.

For example, install the flask framework with the following command:

pip install flask

Command to Uninstall Installed Third-Party Libraries

pip uninstall {Enter third party name here} □

If you want to view the installed libraries, including those that come with the system and those that are installed manually, you only need to execute the command 'pip all'.

More pip parameters and functions can be viewed by entering "pip" on the command line interface.

(2) Condo's management of Python libraries.

Conda can be installed by installing Minconda or Anaconda, which is a simplified version of python and that only contains conda and its dependencies. Conda's management of Python libraries is much the same as pip's. Currently, the main commands that can be used are to install, uninstall and view the installed libraries.

conda {Enter the command here}

For more information about the use of conda, interested readers can use relevant materials from online for study.

With this, we have completed a brief introduction to Python. In the next chapter, we will discuss some of the specialties of Python when compared with other programming languages. We will also learn about the working process of Python in detail in the next chapter. Follow along!

Chapter 2: Differences between Python and other programming languages?

Python is an interpretive, object-oriented and dynamic data type high-level programming language. Since the birth of Python language in the early 1990s, it has gradually been widely used in processing system management tasks and Web programming. Especially with the continuous development of artificial intelligence, Python has become one of the most popular programming languages.

Why is Python special?

There are hundreds of programming languages now available for programmers to start with. However, according to statistics from a survey done by Harvard computer scientists Python is a leading language among beginners. We will in this section discuss about some of the reasons that make Python an understandable language for new programmers.

Python has the following major advantages over other programming languages:

(1) The grammar is concise and clear, and the code is highly readable. Python's syntax requires mandatory indentation, which is used to reflect the logical relationship between statements and significantly improve the readability of the program.

(2) Because it is simple and clear, it is also a programming language with high development efficiency.

(3) Python can be truly cross-platform, for example, the programs we develop can run on Windows, Linux, macOS systems. This is its portability advantage.

(4) It consists of A large number of rich libraries or extensions. Python is often nicknamed glue language. It can easily connect

various modules written in other languages, especially C/C++. Using these abundant third-party libraries, we can easily develop our applications.

(5) The amount of code is small, which improves the software quality to a certain extent. Since the amount of code written in Python is much smaller than that in other languages, the probability of errors is much smaller, which improves the quality of the software written to a certain extent.

Python is very versatile and can be used in the following areas:

(1) web page development;

(2) Visual (GUI) interface development;

(3) Network (can be used for network programming);

(4) System programming;

(5) Data analysis;

(6) Machine learning (Python has various libraries to support it);

(7) Web crawlers (such as those used by Google);

(8) Scientific calculation (Python is used in many aspects of the scientific calculation).

For example, Python is used in many Google services. YouTube is also implemented in Python. The basic framework of the Wikipedia Network initially is also implemented in Python.

How does python work?

Python Program Execution Principle is very simple. We all know that programs written in compiled languages such as C/C++ need to be converted from source files to machine languages used by computers, and then binary executable files are formed after linking by linkers. When running the program, you can load the binary program from the hard disk into memory and run it.

However, for Python, Python source code does not need to be compiled into binary code. It can run programs directly from the source code. The Python interpreter converts the source code into bytecode and then forwards the compiled bytecode to the Python virtual machine (PVM) for execution.

When we run the Python program, the Python interpreter performs two steps.

(1) Compiles Source Code into Byte Code

Compiled bytecode is a Python-specific expression. It is not a binary machine code and needs further compilation before it can be executed by the machine. This is also why Python code cannot run as fast as C/C++.

If the Python process has to write permission on the machine, it will save the bytecode of the program as a file with the extension .pyc. If Python cannot write the bytecode on the machine, the bytecode will be generated in memory and automatically discarded at the end of the program. When building a program, it is best to give Python permission to write on the computer, so as long as the source code is unchanged, the generated .py file can be reused to improve the execution efficiency.

(2) Forwarding the compiled bytecode to Python Virtual Machine (PVM) for execution.

PVM is short for Python Virtual Machine. It is Python's running engine and part of the Python system. It is a large loop that iteratively runs bytecode instructions, completing operations one after another.

In this process, every python program is executed and gives results that can be further analyzed and tested to completely deploy as new applications.

What to look forward to?

As said before, it is always tough to learn a programming language from scratch. Python is one of the most popular programming languages for beginners because it is straight to the point without any deviations. A lot of code is very simple and does what you say. It is comfortably easy for beginners to create predictive logics using python. All we are asking you to do is to stick consistently with python and you can do wonders with it. We recommend you to check GitHub python programs to further increase your interest in Python programming.

In the next chapter, we will in detail discuss about the installation procedure of Python in different operating systems. Let us go!

Chapter 3: How to install Python on your PC?

In the previous chapters, we have discussed Python from a technical and theoretical perspective. From the next chapter, we will start discussing various lexical concepts that make python what it is. Before discussing all those concepts, we need to first install Python in our system. This chapter is a tutorial that explains to you how to install Python in different operating systems. Let us start!

Python Installation and Operation

Due to Python's cross-platform feature, Windows, Linux and macOS systems all support Python's software installation. First of all, we need to download the installation software.

1. Download Python

Here we introduce the installation and operation of Python under the Windows environment. Since there is no built-in Python environment in the Windows operating system, it needs to be installed independently. The installation package can be downloaded from Python's official website (www.Python.org). After opening the official website search for the navigation bar that has a "Downloads" button.

The website recommends a link by default because it can detect your operating system and recommend the latest version of Python 3.x, 3.6.5. After entering the download page of the corresponding version, there is a basic introduction to the environment you are trying to download. Several different versions are mainly aimed at different operating system platforms.

You can choose different files to download according to whether your system is 32-bit or 64-bit.

In the new page that opens, we can find other versions, including the latest test version and the required version 3.4. If you want to install a 64-bit version of 3.6.5, click the framed link on the current page.

At the bottom of the newly opened page, we can find several other links. The file that starts with the Windows entity represents the 64-bit version of Windows, while the file that does not include 64 represents the 32-bit version.

The website shows a compressed installation package (Windows x86-64 Embedded ZipFile), an executable installation file, and a Web-based installation file (Windows x86-64). It is most convenient to download the executable installation package.

Note: 64-bit version cannot be installed on a 32-bit system, but a 32-bit version can be installed on a 32-bit system or 64-bit system.

2. Install Python

The Windows executable installation package is easier to install. Just like installing other Windows applications, we just need to select the appropriate option and click "Next" to complete the installation.

When the options appear in the installation, do not rush to the next step (the system demonstrated here is 64-bit in itself).

It must be noted that after "Add Python3.6 to PATH" is checked and Python 3.6 is added to the environment variable, Python's interactive prompt or Python's commands can be started directly and conveniently at the Windows command prompt in the future.

After selecting "Add Python 3.6 to PATH", select custom installation. Of course, it is also possible to select the first item for installation, which means Python is installed in the user directory of C disk. But at this time, you'd better know what the user directory is so that you can find the installed Python.exe files when necessary in the future.

Proceed with the instructions and python will be installed successfully in the system.

3. Start Python

Python can be started in two ways.

1) Start Python's Own IDLE

If you want to run Python, you can click the "start" button on the Windows desktop and enter "IDLE" in the search box that appears to launch a Python desktop application to quickly provide a prompt of "read-evaluate-print-loop".

IDLE is Python's own simple IDE (Integrated Development Environment), which is Python's graphical interface editor. IDLE can be regarded as a simple version of an integrated development environment. Its function looks simple, but it is helpful for beginners to learn the Python language itself.

Here, a REPL environment is provided, that is, it reads the user's input ("Read"), returns to the car, evaluates and calculates ("Evaluate"), then prints the result ("Print"), and then a prompt "Loop" appears, thus circulating.

2) Start Python at Windows Prompt

Another way to start Python is to run Python programs through the Windows command prompt, and enter "cmd" in the Windows search box (or press "Win+R" key to open the run prompt box, note the "Win" key on the keyboard), or click the start button to enter "cmd" in the pop-up search box and enter to start the Windows command line window.

Note: the flashing cursor after ">" seen here is the command prompt provided by Windows.

When installing Python, since the "Add Python 3.6 to PATH" option is checked and the installed Python is added to the environment variable of Windows, Python can be successfully started by entering "python" after the prompt ">".

The prompt "> > >" indicates that Python installation was successful and Python has been started. The prompt "> > >" is Python-specific.

Next, "print("Hello Python!" is executed in either the first or second startup mode.) ".

If you want to return to the Windows command prompt, you can reach the goal by pressing the shortcut key "Ctrl+Z".

The above two methods are both REPL forms, suitable for writing relatively short programs or commands, and have the advantages of simplicity and flexibility. If the program has more functions and more modules or packages are called, the REPL form is not very convenient to maintain.

In this chapter, we have explained about Installation of Python in detail. In the next chapters, we will start discussing Python syntax in detail. Follow along!

Chapter 4: Python Data types

Python and other programming languages use data types to store values logically in memory. Distinguishing data with values can help operations perform faster. We will also discuss other important programming concepts such as identifiers and reserved keywords in this chapter. Follow along!

Let's start with a detailed discussion of data types.

The operations supported by an object and its description are determined by the data type. Therefore, learning about datatypes is very important for programmers. The Python language provides several built-in data types with rich functions.

Before explaining each data type and its supported operations, the type of the object is usually checked. Python provides a specific built-in function type () to perform these operations. It returns a special type called a type object, which can be divided into other types.

Type detection function [type ()]

Use the type () function to quickly check the type of a variable or to determine the type of operation they can perform.

For example:

type(example)

// Where example =8

We will get the output as int by the type () function.

The Type () function is very simple. It can quickly help us detect the actual type of an object, whether by the name or value of a variable.

Empty object (None)

Another special type in Python is called an empty object. It is just empty and can hold null values.

Simple numeric types

Integer

Integer type (int) is simply an integer, which is used to represent an integer, for example, 100, 2016, etc. Integer literals are represented in four ways: decimal, binary (beginning with "0B" or "0b"), octal (beginning with the number "0") and hexadecimal (beginning with "0X" or "0x").

Python's integer can represent a limited range, which is consistent with the system's maximum integer. For example, the integer on a 32-bit computer is 32 bits, and the range of numbers that can be represented is 231 ~ 2311. Integers on 64-bit computers are 64-bit, and the range of numbers that can be represented is 263 ~ 2631.

Next, look at some examples of integer code, as follows:

first=231283

type(first)

<type 'int'>

first

231283

In the above code, the value of the variable first in line1 code is a binary integer, which belongs to int type. This has been verified in the next lines. Lines 4 to 5 directly output the value of first, and the result is 231283.

Decimal numbers can be converted to binary, octal or hexadecimal using the specified function.

The sample code is as follows:

bin (20) # converts decimal 20 to binary

'0b10100'

oct (20) # converts decimal 20 to octal

'o024'

hex (20) # convert decimal 20 to hexadecimal

'0x14'

Long Integer

Long is a superset of integers, which can represent an infinite integer (actually only limited by the computer's virtual memory size). Long integer literal values are followed by the letters "l" or "l" (uppercase "l" is recommended). Long and integer operations are the same.

The sample code is as follows:

first=13798433*3749803498

<type 'long'>

In the long run, integer and long integer are gradually unified into an integer type. Starting from Python 2.3, integer overflow errors will no longer be reported, and the results will be automatically converted to long integers. Now the two types of integers can be said to be seamlessly combined, and the long integer suffix "L" becomes optional.

Floating point type

Float is used to represent real numbers. For example, 3.14, 9.19, etc. are all floating-point types. Floating-point literals can be expressed in decimal or scientific notation.

The scientific notation in Python is expressed as follows:

< real number > e or e < integer >

Wherein, e or e represents a base of 10, the following integer represents an index, and the positive and negative of the index are expressed by+or, where+can be omitted. For example, 1.34E3 means 1.34x103 and 1.5E−3 means 1.5x10-3.

The sample code is as follows:

> > 1.2e5 # floating-point number is 1.2×105

One hundred and twenty thousand

Boolean type

The boolean type can be regarded as a special integer. Boolean data has only two values: True and False, corresponding to 1 and 0 of integer respectively. Every Python object is inherently boolean (True or False), which can then be used in boolean tests (such as if, while).

User-defined class instances that return 0 or False if methods nonzero () or len () are defined. Boolean values of all objects except the above objects are True. This section involves a lot of knowledge explained later. All you need to know here is that Boolean values can only be True and False.

plural

The complex number type is used to represent the complex number in mathematics. For example, 5+3j and −3.4−6.8j are all complex number types. The plural type in Python is a data type that is not available in general computer languages.

It has the following two characteristics:

(1) Complex numbers consist of real numbers and imaginary numbers, which are expressed as real+imagj or real+imagJ.

(2) The real part and imaginary part imag of complex numbers are both floating-point types.

It should be noted that a complex number must have real numbers and j representing imaginary parts, e.g. 1j and 1j are complex numbers, and 0.0 is not a complex number, and the real part representing imaginary parts cannot be omitted even if it is 1.

Example codes for complex numbers are as follows:

sample = 6+2j

sample

(6+2j)

sample.real # real part

One

type(sample.real)

<class 'float'>

sample.imag # imaginary part

Two

type(sample.imag)

<class 'float'>

Identifiers and keywords

identifier

In real life, people often use some names to mark things. For example, each fruit has a name to mark.

Similarly, if you want to express something in a program, you need developers to customize some symbols and names, which are called identifiers. For example, variable names, function names, etc. are identifiers.

The identifier in Python consists of letters, numbers and underscore "_", and its naming method needs to follow certain rules, as follows.

(1) Identifiers consist of letters, underscores, and numbers, and cannot begin with numbers.

The sample code is as follows:

FromNo12 # legal identifier

From#12 # is an illegal identifier. Identifiers cannot contain # symbols.

2ndObj # is an illegal identifier. Identifiers cannot start with a number.

(2) Identifiers in Python are case sensitive. For example, andy and Andy are different identifiers.

(3) Identifiers in Python cannot use keywords. For example, if cannot be used as an identifier.

Also, to standardize the naming of identifiers, the following suggestions are made on the naming of identifiers.

(1) Knowing the meaning by name: give a meaningful name and try your best to know what the identifier means at a glance, thus improving the readability of the code. For example, the definition name is represented by name, and the definition student is represented by student.

(2) When naming variables, many computer languages suggest hump naming. However, hump naming is not recommended in Python.

keywords

In Python, identifiers with special functions are called keywords. The keyword is already used by Python itself, and developers are not allowed to define identifiers with the same name as the keyword.

The keywords in Python each represent a different meaning. If you want to view the keyword information, you can enter the help () command to enter the help system to view.

The sample code is as follows:

> > > help () # enter the help system

Help> keywords # view all keyword lists

Help> return # view the description of the keyword return

Help > quit # to exit the help system

With this we have completed a brief explanation to data types and in the next chapter we will explain about variables in detail. Follow along!

Chapter 5: Python Variables

Programming is a tough task and it requires hard work to master various topics. Programmers are destined to know about how computers store data. This will make it easy to understand their resources and successfully pool data types to create favorable applications. This may seem silly for programs with fewer lines of code but when you are using advanced third-party libraries to create complex applications this will become essential. In the previous chapter we have talked about data types in detail and in this chapter we will in detail discuss variables that store data for repetitive usage.

Variables

In real life, when we buy things in supermarkets, we often need to use shopping carts to store items. After all, after items are purchased, we can check out at the cash register.

Let's imagine, if you want to sum up multiple data in the program, you need to store the data first and then add up the data.

In Python, variables are needed to store data. Variables can be understood as shopping carts used for shopping in supermarkets, and their types and values are initialized at the moment of assignment. The assignment of variables is represented by an equal sign, and the example code is shown below. We will also discuss in detail about Assignment operation in the next chapter.

Num1 = 257 # Num1 is a variable, just like a shopping cart, which stores data 257

Num2 = 87 # Num2 is also a variable, and the stored data is 87

Result = num1+num2 # Accumulates the data in the two "shopping carts" num1 and num2 and then puts them into the result variable

In the above example, num1, num2, and result are variables. Among them, variables num1 and num2 are just like a shopping cart, and the data they store are 257 and 87 respectively. The data stored in the variable result is the cumulative sum of the data in the two "shopping carts" num1 and num2.

Types of Variables

Variables are used to store data, so have you ever thought about how much space we should let variables take up and what kind of data to store? Before explaining the types of variables, let's take a look at an example of life.

For example, we need to transport a computer. Large trucks and cars can be completed. However, if we use a large truck to transport a computer, it is a little fussy and wastes the space of a large truck.

Similarly, if variables are used to store data, in order to make full use of memory space, we can specify different types for variables.

(1) Number Type

Number types in Python include integer, floating-point, and complex types.

The sample code is as follows:

x = 1

x = 3.232

x = 5.65f

(2) Boolean type

Boolean type is a special integer with only two values, True and False. If a Boolean value is evaluated numerically, True will be treated as integer 1 and False as integer 0.

(3) String Type

A string in Python is defined as a collection of characters that are enclosed in quotation marks, which can be single, double quotation marks, or triple quotation marks (three consecutive single quotation marks or double quotation marks). The string has index rules, the index of the first character is 0, the index of the second character is 1, and so on.

The following is a sample code for a string:

Str1='God'

Str2="This is great"

Str3="'You are lost'"

(4) List and tuple type

We can think of lists and tuples as ordinary "arrays". They can hold any number of values of any type, which are called elements. The difference is that the elements in the list are contained in brackets []. The number and value of elements can be modified at will. The elements in the tuple are contained in parentheses (). Elements cannot be modified.

Let's look at the representation of lists and tuples.

A list = [1,768,' lost'] # This is a list

A tuple = (1,2464,' great') # This is a tuple

(5) dictionary type

Dictionary is a mapping data type in Python and consists of key-value pairs. Dictionaries can store different types of elements, which are contained in braces {}. In general, the keys of the dictionary will be expressed in the form of strings or numbers, and the values can be of any type.

The sample code is as follows:

Sample = {"name": "Rob", "age": 67} # this is a dictionary

In the above code, the variable Sample is a dictionary type, which stores two elements, the key of the first element is a name, and the value is Rob. The key of the second element is age with a value of 67.

In Python, as long as a variable is defined and the variable stores data, the data type of the variable is already determined. This is because the system will automatically identify the data type of the variable, and there is no need for developers to explicitly specify the data type of the variable.

If you want to view the type of a variable, you can use "Type" (the name of the variable).

The sample code is as follows:

>>> dude = 5.234

> > > type (dude)//use the type function to view types

```
<type 'float'>
```

In the above code, the value stored in the variable num is 5.234, and the system will automatically judge the data type of num variable as float according to the value. Therefore, when viewing the data type of variable num using the type function, the result is float.

In the next section, we will discuss some of the syntactical rules to be followed while writing code such as comments and sentence wrapping.

What are comments in Python?

The single-line comment in Python starts with #, and the sample code is as follows:

```
# This is the start
print ("Hello, This is the end!" ) # Second comment
```

A multiline comment can use three quotation marks as the opening and closing symbols, and the three quotation marks can be three single quotation marks or three double quotation marks. For example, when entering the declaration file of the print function, the relevant explanations of the print function are all annotated with three quotation marks.

```
''' Comment here ''' # Single quotation comment
""" Comment here """ # Double quotation comment
```

Lines and indents

Python's most important and well-discussed ability is that it uses different forms of indentation, without using braces {}.

The sample code is as follows:

if {Enter the Boolean entity here}

Print ("This is right") # Get use of a placeholder

else:

Print ("This is wrong") # Get use of a placeholder

The above program is indented with an inconsistent number of spaces, which will lead to running errors.

 if {Enter the Boolean entity here}

 print ("get this")

 print ("This is right")

else:

 print ("Do this")

PRINT ("This is wrong") # Inconsistent indentations will result in running errors

Due to inconsistent indentation of the above programs, indentation error will appear after execution.

Note:

(1) For a person who uses indentation as a code block for the first time, he may be confused about the width of indentation. Here, we recommend using 4 spaces.

(2) Tabs represent different blank widths in different text editors. If the code we use is to be used across platforms, it is recommended that you do not use tabs.

Sentence Wrapping

Python usually writes a statement one line at a time, but if it is syntactically too long, it needs line wrapping, which can be implemented by adding a pair of parentheses to the outside of the statement.

Now we are ready to give a brief explanation about various essential programming operations in the next chapter. Let us start with it!

Chapter 6: Basic operation of Python Language

In the previous chapters, we have discussed various lexical concepts that are necessary to write efficient code. In this chapter, we will discuss various operations that made Python a popular language. This is a comprehensive chapter and introduces you to a lot of concepts in detail. Let us start!

What is a statement?

When a variable is declared, an expression is used to create and process the object. If some logical control is added, a statement is formed. It can also be said that statements contain expressions, so statements are the most basic infrastructure for Python programs.

Python Assignment Statement

Learning assignment statements in Python makes it easier to learn the other statements. Learning Python assignment statement is mainly to master and understand its logic.

1. Assignment statement

The essence of assignment statements in Python is to create a reference to an object.

There are mainly the following methods of an assignment.

a) Basic assignment method

☐ "first=5"

This is equivalent to creating a variable first that points to the object 5 stored in memory. "first=5" is an assignment statement. After performing the assignment operation, you can print or display the value of first at will.

2) Understand assignment logic

When declaring variables, there are at least two parts, one is the variable table used to store variable names, and the other is the memory storage area [4,6].

When "first=5" is declared, the system first opens a storage space in the memory area, stores the value 5, and then points the variable first to the object 5 stored in the memory, which is equivalent to having the object 5 first in the memory storage area. Then first appears in the variable table, and points to 5. This point can also be called "reference".

Although the syntax of assignment statements is simple, please carefully understand the assignment logic in Python. This kind of assignment logic affects all aspects of Python. If you understand assignment logic, you can better understand and write Python programs.

If you have programming experience in C language, you will know that variables in C programs hold value, while variables in Python point to a value. Variables exist only as a reference relationship and no longer have storage functions. In Python, each data occupies a memory space, and data is called an object in Python.

An integer 5 is an int object, a' hello' is a string object, and a [1, 2, 3] is a list object.

In Python, you can use the global built-in function id(obj) to obtain the id of an object as the storage address of the object in memory. The global built-in function is used directly and does not need to refer to any package.

☐ Note: The change of address before and after variable first indicates that the variable points to the object!

After an object is created, it cannot be destroyed directly. Therefore, in the above example, the variable a points to the object 5 first, and then continues to execute "a=a+5", which produces a new object 10. Since the object 5 cannot be destroyed, let A point to the new object 10 instead of overwriting the object 5 with the object 10. After the code execution is completed, there are still objects 5 and 10 in the memory, but the variable A points to the new object 10.

If no variable points to object 5 (it cannot be referenced), Python will use a garbage collection mechanism to decide whether to recycle it (this is automatic and does not require the programmer to worry about it).

There is a garbage collection mechanism inside Python. The garbage collection mechanism detects that if no variable references an object within a specific time, the object will be collected, releasing the resources it occupies.

There is a reference counter inside Python, and the garbage collection mechanism judges whether an object has a reference according to the reference counter, to decide whether to automatically release the resources occupied by the object. The garbage collection mechanism targets unreferenced objects in Python and is inferred from a result obtained by a reference counter.

This understanding is also very important. When we talk about data types such as lists in the future, we will see again the importance of correctly understanding the variable pointing to the object.

Multi-objective assignment

The multi-objective assignment is a way of assigning the same value to multiple variables.

☐ Enhanced assignment or parameterized assignment

Sometimes it is desirable to replace the original value of a variable by re-assigning it after doing an operation based on its original value.

☐ **Exchange the values of two variables.**

In other languages, such as Java, C, C++, etc., at least three lines of code are required to exchange the values of two variables, while in Python, only one line of code is required to exchange the values of two variables.

Before introducing other Python statements, let us look at the sequential execution and basic input and output in Python process control.

Sequential execution is the default code execution method in process control and is relatively simple. The basic principle is that the sequence of code execution is consistent with the sequence of program code writing.

The program execution order is consistent with the writing order.

The data in the above program is fixed in the program, but sometimes it may be necessary for programmers or software users to input some data into the program during the operation of the program, which requires input functions.

input () function

Input on the console is realized through the global function input (). The input () function receives information input from the console by the user. The default type is a str character type, which can be converted into specific data types as required.

If you want to give the user some hints when inputting data, you can pass in a parameter with hints in the input () function!

eval () function

The eval () function evaluates str character data as a valid expression and returns the result. Simply put, it is to remove the quotation marks at the left and right ends of the string.

print () function

The print () function here simply outputs the value of an object or variable. The print () function has some commonly used parameters, which are very flexible to use in actual development.

If you want to use a special line of characters to separate the output of the front and back lines, such as 20 "=" to separate the output of the front and back lines, you can use "print("="*20)" to achieve the goal.

☐ 1) Multiple variables are output on one line, separated by spaces by default Outputs multiple contents separated by commas on one line, with the separator being a space.

2) Multiple variables are output on one line, and the separator between them is changed

If you want the output to be separated by other separators, you can write a delimiter statement. Any character can be used as the delimiter here, that is, the print () function can specify the delimiter manually.

Multiple lines of print () function output on one line

In the parameter table of the print () function, there is a parameter "end" that specifies the termination symbol. by default, it is a line break, that is, "end='\n'". Therefore, the output of multiple print statements can be output on one line by specifying a terminator.

☐ The default delimiter for the print () function is a space, and the terminating symbol is a newline' \n'. After understanding the above contents, the flexibility of output will be greatly improved in actual development.

Digital print format

Specify the format or number of digits of the output number by formatting the string.

1) Outputs decimals of specified digits

☐ In the print format, the ':' in curly brackets indicates that the value appearing at the current position is formatted, and the' .2f' indicates that the following value is output as floating-point, but only 2 decimal places are reserved, and the third digit is rounded.

2) output a fixed width value

If you want to specify the width of the overall digital output, the form is as follows:

width {Enter value}

☐ Note:' {:12, .2f}' means the total width, which is aligned to the right by default, with not enough digits, and is preceded by a space; ", "means thousands separator; ".2f" means keeping 2 decimal places.

☐ Because sometimes it is necessary to output multiple lines of content on the console, and each line has multiple columns, but each line has a length and a short length. If you want to typeset more neatly, you can use this method at this time.

For more usage of the print () function, please refer to it through the help(print) command.

With this, we have completed a comprehensive chapter that explained to us a lot of python programming concepts. In the next chapter, we will in detail discuss modules that give interactivity to python. Let us go!

Chapter 7: Interactivity in Python

Python is a thorough language that utilizes a lot of components. However, you need to remember that one of the most important reasons for the success of Python is its interactivity. Every programming language provides interactivity using different methodologies. Python is however known to provide interactivity with the help of modules and packages. In this chapter, we will discuss these functions in detail along with a lot of examples. Follow along!

How Modules provide interactivity?

In Python, the import keyword can be used to introduce a module. For example, the math module can be introduced and import math can be used.

The basic format for introducing modules using import is as follows:

import firstmodule,secondmodule...

At this time, if the module is located at that same location, the module will be imported automatically.

If you want to call a function in a module, you must reference it like this:

Module Name. {Enter the name of the function}

When calling a function in a module, the module name is added because there may be functions with the same name in multiple modules. At this time, if only the function name is used to call, the interpreter cannot know which function to call. Therefore, if a module is introduced as described above, the calling function must be added with the module name.

Specific examples are as follows:

import math

This is said to be wrong

print(sqrt(12))

Only in this way can the results be correctly output

print({Enter the module here}.sqrt(12))

Sometimes we only need to use a certain function in the module, and only need to introduce the function. At this time, the following format can be applied:

from {Name of the entity} import function name 1, function name 2 ..

For your clear understanding here is an instance:

from fib import {Enter the Fibonacci instance here}

When introducing a function in this way, only the function name and not the module name can be given when calling the function, but when two modules contain functions with the same name, the latter introduction will cover the previous introduction.

That is to say, if there is a function function in module A, there is also a function function in module B. If the function in A is introduced before the function in B, then when the function is called, the function in module B is executed.

You can also use the following statement for invoking all statements at once.

From module name import *

It should be noted that although Python provides a simple method to import all items in a module you should use other invoking statements too.

When we use import to introduce a module, how does the Python interpreter find the corresponding file?

This involves Python's search path, which consists of a series of directory names, from which Python interpreter searches for the introduced modules in turn.

The search path is determined when Python is compiled or installed, and the installation of the new library should also be modified.

The search operation to the PATH variable in the sys module is used, and can be verified by code as follows:

import provider

print(provider.path)

Now, create a fibo.py file in the interpreter's current directory or a directory in sys.path, with the following sample code:

fibonacci Sequence Module

deffib (n): # fibonacci sequence defined to n

first, second = 0, 1

while second < n:

print(second, end=' ')

first, second = second, first+second

print()

def fib2 (n): # Fibonacci sequence returned to n

result = []

first, second = 0, 1

while second < n:

result.append(second)

first, second = second, first+second

return result

Then enter the Python interpreter and import this module using the following command:

import fibo

In doing so, the name of the function directly defined in fibo is not written into the current symbol table, but the name of the module fibo is written there. You can use the module name to access the function, with the following sample code:

import fibo

fibo.fib(1000)

fibo.fib2(100)

fibo.__name__

If you plan to use a function frequently, you can assign it to a local name.

The example code is as follows:

fib=fibo.fib

fib(500)

□ *Module production*

In Python, each Python file can be used as a module, and the name of the module is the name of the file. At this time, if you want to use the test.py file in the main.py file, you can use "from test import add" to introduce it.

Example main.py

```
from test import add

result = test.add(11,22)

print(result)
```

In actual development, after a developer has written a module, to make the module achieve the desired effect in the project, the developer will add some test information to the py file.

At this time, if this file is introduced into other py files, think about whether the code tested will also execute? The test file is introduced into main.py the sample code is as follows:

As can be seen from the above results, the test code in test.py is also running. However, this is not reasonable. Test code should only be run when test.py is executed separately, and should not be executed when referenced by other files.

To solve this problem, Python provides a special attribute. Each module has a special attribute. when its value is' __main__', it indicates that the module itself is running, otherwise, it is referenced. Therefore, if we want a program block in the module not to execute when the module is introduced, we can do so by judging the value of the __name__ attribute.

Packages

To organize the modules well, multiple modules are usually put into one package. The package is the directory where Python module files are located, and __init__.py files must exist under the directory (the file contents can be empty).

At this time, if main.py wants to reference module_a1 in package_a, it can be implemented with the following statement:

```
from package_a import module_a1

import package_a.module_a1
```

With this, we have completed a brief explanation of interactivity in python using modules. In the next chapter, we will talk about structures in detail. Follow along!

Chapter 8: Structures in Python

Python is a structural language and provides various structures to store and manipulate data for performing operations. In this chapter, we will in detail discuss structures such as lists. A lot of this chapter is theoretical and needs an understanding of various concepts explained before. Let us start!

What is a list?

The string data type learned earlier can be used to store a single piece string of information. But Suppose if there are 100 students in a class. If you want to store the names of all the students in this class, you need to define 100 variables, and each variable stores one student's name.

However, if there are 1,000 students or more, what should we do?

You are lucky because structures such as lists can solve the above problem. A list is a data structure in Python that can store different types of data. The way to create the list is very simple, just use square brackets to enclose the different data items separated by commas.

The sample code is as follows:

A = [1,'Tom','a', [2, 'b']]

As the index of strings, the list index starts from 0. We can access the values in the list by subscript index.

Example Accessing List Elements Using Indexes

A = ['Tom', 'Sam', 'Ram']

print(A[0])

```
print(A[1])
```

```
print(A[2])
```

In Example, an index is used to access elements in the list, where the index of the first element is 0, the index of the second element is 1, and so on.

To output each data of the list more efficiently, we can use the for and while loops to traverse the output list.

The following is a case study to illustrate how to loop through the list using for and while.

1. Use the for loop to traverse the list

The way to use the for loop to traverse the list is very simple, just need to traverse the list as a sequence in the for-loop expression.

Next, a case will be presented to understand this scenario.

```
getdetails = ['Sam','Tom','Ram']
```

```
for name in getdetails:
```

```
print(name)
```

In Example, when using the for loop to traverse the list, since the list is originally a sequence, the names list can be directly used as the sequence of the for-loop expression to obtain the elements in the list one by one.

2. Use while loop to traverse the list

To use the while loop to traverse the list, first, you need to obtain the length of the list, and use the obtained list length as the condition of the while loop.

Next, a case will be presented, as shown in Example.

Example: Uses the while loop to traverse the list

```
getdetails = ['Sam','Tom','Ram']
```

```
length = len(namesList)
```

```
first = 0
```

```
while first<length:
```

```
print(namesList[first])
first+=1
```

In Example, when using the while loop to traverse the list, because the while loop needs to specify the number of traversals, it is necessary to use the len function to obtain the length of the list, that is, the number of elements to traverse.

List Common Operations

Add Elements to the List

There are many ways to add elements to the list, as follows:

(1) You can add elements to the list through append.

(2) extend allows you to add elements from another list to the list one by one.

(3) insert the element object before the specified position index by insert(index, object).

Next, we will demonstrate the use of these methods through case studies as follows.

1. Add elements to the list by append

Elements added to the list using append are at the end of the list. Next, we will demonstrate it through a case, as shown in Example.

```
# Prompt and Add Element
temp = input ('please enter the name of the student to be added:')
A.append(temp)
```

In the example, the program uses append to add an element at the end of the list and uses for loop to traverse the list before and after adding the element, respectively, to verify whether the element in the list was added successfully.

2. Add elements to the list through extend

Use extend to add all elements from one list to another. Next, a case will be presented.

Examples Use extend to Add List Elements

first = [1, 2]

second = [3, 4]

first.append(second)

print(first)

first.extend(second)

print(first)

In Examples, append is used to add List first to the end of List second, and then extend is used to add all the elements of List B to List A.

3. Add elements to the list by insert

Use insert to add an element at a specified location in the list. Next, a case will be presented, as shown in Example.

Example Use insert to insert an element into a list

sample = [0, 1, 2]

sample.insert(1, 3)

print(sample)

In Example, the second line of code uses insert to add an element 3 to the list at index 1.

Find Elements in List

The so-called lookup is to see if the specified element exists. Common operators for lookup in Python are explained below.

(1)in (present): if present, the result is True; otherwise, it is False.

(2)not in: If it does not exist, the result is True, otherwise it is False.

Next, a case is used to demonstrate how to find elements in the list.

Example Finding Elements in a List

findName = input ('please enter the name you want to find:')

look for existence

if findName in {Enter entity details here}

In the example, through the traversal of the list, find out whether the specified element exists in the list. After the program is run, two kinds of results will be generated, and the results of these two operations are shown.

Delete Elements from the List

In real life, if a student changes classes, then the transferred student information should be deleted. The deletion function is often used in development. There are three common deletion methods for list elements, as follows.

(1)del: Delete according to subscript.

(2)pop: Take away the end element

(3)remove: Remove according to the value of the element.

Next, we will demonstrate the use of the above three deletion methods through cases as follows.

1. Use del to delete the list

Del can be used to delete the entire list. Next, we will demonstrate it through a case.

Examples Use del to Delete Elements in a List

del movieName[2]

2. Use pop to delete list elements

Pop can be used to delete the last element of the list. Next, a case will be presented.

movieName.pop()

3. Use remove to remove list elements

Use remove to remove a specified element of the list. Next, we will demonstrate it through a case.

movieName.remove ('lord of the rings')

Sorting Operation of List

If you want to rearrange the elements in the list, you can use the sort or reverse method. Among them, the sort method rearranges the elements in the list in a specific order. The reverse method is to reverse the list. Next, a case is used to demonstrate the use of these two methods.

Example: Sorting Operation of List

sample = [1, 4, 2, 3]

sample.reverse()

sample.sort()

print(sample)

In the example, the second line of codes arranges the list in reverse order, the fourth line of codes arranges the list recursively, and the sixth line of codes arranges the list from large to small.

With this, we have completed various operations that structures can perform. In the next chapter, we will in detail discuss functions with various examples. Let us go!

Chapter 9: Functions in Python

This chapter is a comprehensive guide about functions. We will look at various components of function with examples. Let us go!

What is a Function?

Functions are organized and reusable code segments used to implement single or associated functionalities, which can improve the modularity of applications and the reuse rate of codes. Python provides many built-in functions, such as print (). Also, we can create our own functions, that is, custom functions.

Next, look at a code:

// display(" * ")

// display(" *** ")

// display("*****")

If you need to output the above graphics in different parts of a program, it is not advisable to use the print () function to output each time. To improve writing efficiency and code reusability, we can organize code blocks with independent functions into a small module, which is called a function.

Defining Functions

We can define a function to achieve the desired functionality. Python definition functions begin with def, and the basic format for defining functions is as follows:

Def function {Enter the name here} (Enter parameters here):

"//Use this to define function String"

Function { Body}

Return expression

Note that if the parameter list contains more than one parameter, by default, the parameter values and parameter names match in the order defined in the function declaration.

Next, define a function that can complete printing information, as shown in Example below.

Example : Functions of Printing Information

```
# defines a function that can print information.
def Useforprint():
print('----------------------------------')
print ('life is short, I use python')
print('----------------------------------')
```

Call Function

After defining a function, it is equivalent to having a piece of code with certain methods. To make these codes executable, you need to call it. Calling a function is very simple. You can call it by "function name ()".

For example, the code that calls the Useforprint function in the above section is as follows:

After the function is defined, the function will not be executed automatically and needs to be called

Useforprint()

Parameters of Function

Before introducing the parameters of the function, let's first solve a problem. For example, it is required to define a function that is used to calculate the sum of two numbers and print out the calculated results. Convert the above requirements into codes.

The sample codes are as follows:

```
def thisisaddition():
 result = 62+12
 print(result)
```

The functionality of the above function is to calculate the sum of 62 and 12. At this time, no matter how many times this function is called, the result will always be the same, and only the sum of two fixed numbers can be calculated, making this function very limited.

To make the defined function more general, that is, to calculate the sum of any two numbers, two parameters can be added when defining the function, and the two parameters can receive the value passed to the function.

Next, a case is used to demonstrate how a function passes parameters.

Example: Function Transfer Parameters

defines a function that receives 2 parameters

def thisisaddition(first, second):

third = first+second

print(third)

In Example, a function capable of receiving two parameters is defined. Where first is the first parameter for receiving the first value passed by the function; the second is the second parameter and receives the second value passed by the function. At this time, if you want to call the thisisaddition function, you need to pass two numeric values to the function's parameters.

The example code is as follows:

When calling a function with parameters, you need to pass data in parentheses.

thisisaddition(62, 12)

It should be noted that if a function defines multiple parameters, then when calling the function, the passed data should correspond to the defined parameters one by one.

Default Parameters

When defining a function, you can set a default value for its parameter, which is called the default parameter. When calling a function, because the default parameter has been assigned a value at the time of definition, it can be directly ignored, while other parameters must be passed in values. If the default parameter does not have an incoming value, the default value is directly used. If the default parameter passes in value, the new value passed in is used instead.

Next, we use a case to demonstrate the use of the default parameter.

Example : Default Parameters

```
def getdetails( input, time = 35 ):
# prints any incoming string
print("Details:", input)
print("Time:", time)
# calls printinfo function
printinfo(input="sydney" )
printinfo(input="sydney",time=2232)
```

In an example, lines 1-4 define the getdetails function with two parameters. Among them, the input parameter has no default value, and age has already set the default value as the default parameter.

When calling the getdetails function, because only the value of the name parameter is passed in, the program uses the default value of the age parameter. When the getdetails function is called on line 7, the values of the name and age parameters are passed in at the same time, so the program will use the new value passed to the age parameter.

It should be noted that parameters with default values must be located at the back of the parameter list. Otherwise, the program will report an error, for example, add parameter sex to the getdetails function and place it at the back of the parameter list to look at the error information.

With this, we have completed a thorough explanation of functions in python. In the next section, we will discuss different types of functions with an example.

Chapter 10: How to create own functions?

In this chapter, we are going to discuss various types of functions in detail. We will also in detail discuss user made functions with the help of an example.

According to whether there are parameters and return values, functions can be roughly divided into four types:

(1) The functions that have no parameters and no return value.

(2) The functions that have no parameters but returns a value.

(3) The function that has parameters but that doesn't return a value.

(4) Functions that have parameters and return values.

Next, the four types will be explained in detail.

Functions without Parameters and Return Values

Functions with no parameters and no return value can neither receive parameters nor return values.

Next, the use of this type of function is demonstrated by a function that prints prompts, as shown in Example.

Example: Functions Without Parameters and Return Values

def printresults():

// This is your place to choose

// display('Order your items here')

{ Now enter the output required for the entities}

printresults()

Functions with No Parameters but Returns Values

This type of function cannot receive parameters, but it can return some data. Generally, this type of function is used when collecting data. Next, we will demonstrate through an example.

Example: Functions with No Parameters but Returns Values

This will give temperature

def result():

Here are some processing procedures for obtaining temperature.

For the sake of simplicity, the simulation returns a data first.

 return 54

 usage = useresults()

print ('This is your body result', usage)

Functions with Parameters and No Return Value

In actual development, functions with parameters and no return value are rarely used. Because with functions as function modules and with parameters passed in, the return value is expected to be used in most cases. Here, everyone can know something about functions with parameters and no return value.

The example code is as follows:

```
// function
def send(usecase1,usecase2):
result=usecase1+usecase2
print ('calculated as: %d' %result)
```

Functions with Parameters and Return Values

Such functions can not only receive parameters but also return certain data. In general, such functions can be used for applications that process data and require results. Next, we will demonstrate it through a case.

Example: Functions with Parameters and Return Values

```
# calculates the cumulative sum of 1 ~ num
while i<=usetheresult:
result = result + i
i+=1
```

In the next section, we will describe user-made functions and will further explain the concept of user-made functions using a thorough example.

What is a user-made function?

A user made function is a function that creates a function with its parameters and logic. We usually have system functions such as print(), math() to solve a lot of day-to-day problems. User-made functions are usually used for repetitive tasks. In the next section, we will introduce you to a business card manager application that uses various user-made functions. Follow along to understand the essence of functions in programming.

Function Case- Business Card Manager

Business card manager is a practical software for life, which is used to help manage all business cards in mobile phones. To help people learn how to choose four types of functions in practical application, we develop a business card manager.

This case requires the use of functions to complete various functions, and according to the keyboard input to select the corresponding function to complete these functions.

There are six functions in the business card management menu, and the function selected by the user is responded by receiving the serial number input by the keyboard. Once the user enters "6", he will quit the business card management system.

First of all, Create a project and create a Python file named "Business Card Management System". The specific implementation steps are as follows.

1. Output the menu of the Business Card Manager

Considering that this function is only used to output information and the output content is fixed, a function displayMenu () with no parameters and no return value is defined as follows.

def display():

print("-"*60)

{ Enter the menu entities here}

print("-"*60)

Use the while loop to output menu information without interruption. To test the above menu function as soon as possible, the number of cycles is limited to 1, as follows.

first = 0

while first<1:

Print menu

display()

Run the program and the console outputs the above menu information.

2. Obtain the information input by the user

After the menu is displayed, the user enters the serial number to be executed according to the prompt. The input () function receives the user's selection from the keyboard and returns the selected sequence number, so a function useinput() with no parameters and a return value is defined as follows.

Get the information entered by the user

def useinput():

 storedvalue = input ("please enter the selected serial number:")

 return int(storedvalue)

After the while loop prints the menu, call the useinput () function to obtain the information entered by the user, as follows.

Waiting for User Selection

present = useinput()

Run the program and the console outputs the information.

☐ *3. Perform different functions by obtaining serial numbers*

After obtaining the serial number, perform the corresponding operation according to the serial number. At the end of the while statement, use the if-Elif statement to complete the corresponding functions according to the sequence number selected by the user, as follows.

if present == 1:

 pass

elif present == 2:

 {Use the remaining conditional entities here}

 print ("Incorrect input, please re-enter ...")

Next, the function corresponding to the serial number will be processed under each condition. Here, only the functions of "Add Business Card" and "Query Business Card" will be introduced.

4. Add Business Cards

To save all business card information, you need a list. Before the while statement, define an empty list as follows.

namespresent = []

The user has selected serial number 1, and should be prompted to enter his name and then add it to the above empty list. Therefore, we define a function with no parameters and no return value, as follows.

Add Business Cards

def enterInf():

 enterInf = input ("please enter name:")

 enterinf.append(newName)

Then, when the user selects the serial number 1, the above method is called to realize the function of adding business cards, as follows.

 if present == 1:

 enterInf()

elif present == 2:

Run the program and the console will output the information.

5.Check the information about all business cards

The user has selected serial number 5. At this time, all the name information should be obtained from the list and printed in a fixed format. Therefore, we define a function with parameters and no return value, as follows.

```python
# View information for all business cards
def getallnames(structure):
    print("="*60)
    for info in structure:
        print(info)
    print("="*60)
```

Then, when the user selects the serial number 5, the above method is called to realize the function of viewing all business cards, as follows.

```python
elif present == 4:
    pass
elif present == 5:
    getallnames(nameList)
```

Run the program and the console will output the information.

With this, we have completed a brief explanation about user-made functions in Python. In the next chapter, we will start discussing conditional and loop statements in detail. Let us go!

Chapter 11: Conditional and Loops in Python?

In this chapter, we will learn in detail about conditional and loop statements. Before discussing these statements, we need to learn about judgment the essential concept required to master these concepts.

What is the judgment?

Judgment means that only when certain conditions are met one can be allowed to do something, while when the conditions are not met, one is not allowed to do it. For example, in real life, crossing the road depends on traffic lights. If it is a green light, you can cross the road, otherwise, you need to stop and wait.

Judgment is used not only in life but also in program development. For example, when a user logs in, only if the user name and password are all correct, he can be allowed to log in. Python provides many kinds of judgment statements. In the next section, we will explain these judgment statements in detail.

If statement

The if statement is the simplest conditional judgment statement. It can control the execution process of the program.

Its format is as follows:

If criteria:

Things to do when you meet the first condition.

Things to do when you meet the second condition

...

...

Things to be done when conditions are not met at all

In the above format, the following statement can be executed only if the judgment condition is satisfied.

□ To help people better understand the use of if statements, next, we will demonstrate the function of if statements through two cases, as follows.

Example:

//if statement -1

age=30

Print ("if judgment starts")

if age>=22:

Print ("This is true")

Print ("-if judgment ends")

In Example, the output of the program is different only if the value of the age variable is different. From this, we can see the function of if judgment statement that is: only when certain conditions are met the specified code will be executed, otherwise, it will not be executed.

Note:

1. Use a colon (:) after each if condition to indicate that the following statement is to be executed after the condition is met.

2. Use indents to divide statement blocks. Statements with the same number of indents together form a statement block.

3. There is no switch-case statement in Python.

if-else statement

When using if, it can only do what it wants to do when it meets the conditions. If it does not meet the conditions and needs to do something, what should it do? to counter this problem We can use if-else statements.

If-else statements are used in the following format:

If condition:

Things to do when you meet the first condition

Things to do when you meet the second condition.

...

Things to be done when nth conditions are met

else:

Things to do when the first conditions are not met

Things to do when second conditions are not met

...

Things to do when nth conditions are not met

To help people better understand the use of if-else statements, next, we will demonstrate the function of if-else statements through a case.

Example if-else statement

Ticket = 1 # with 1 for tickets, 0 for no tickets

if ticket == 1:

  print ("you can get on the train if you have a ticket")

  print ("I can finally see home")

else:

print ("No tickets, no boarding")

print ("Dear, I'll see you next time")

Set the value of the variable ticket to 0 and run the program again.

You will understand about conditional statements in depth if you can practice it by practical coding.

If nesting

When we take a train or subway, we have to buy a ticket first. Only when we buy a ticket, we can enter the station for security checks. Only when we pass the security check, we can take the bus normally. In the process of taking a train or subway, the latter judgment condition is based on the previous judgment. Given this situation, if nesting can be used.

If nesting refers to the inclusion of an if or if-else statement in an if or if-else statement, and its nesting format is as follows:

if conditions1:

{// What to do if condition 1 is met

 // things that meet condition 1

if conditions2:

things are done to meet condition 2

}

In the above format, we can choose whether to use if statement or if-else statement for the if of the outer layer and if of the inner layer according to the actual development.

Loop Statements

In real life, there are many cyclic procedures. For example, the alternation of traffic lights is a repetitive process. In the program, if you want to repeat some operations, you can use circular statements also called loops. Python provides two loop statements, the while loop and the for loop. We will now in detail discuss these two statements.

While loop

The basic format of the while loop is as follows:

While

{ Enter the logic

  Output results

}

If the condition is satisfied, the loop statement is executed.

When the conditional expression is True, the program executes a loop statement.

It should be noted that in the while loop, colon and indentation should also be noted. Also, there is no do-while loop in Python.

If we want the loop to be infinite, we can implement an infinite loop by setting the conditional expression to always be True. An infinite loop is very useful for real-time requests from clients on the server.

Next, a case is used to demonstrate the specific code.

Example: while loop

value = 1

While value == 1 :

expression is always True

 input = int(give ("enter a number:"))

 print ("The number you entered is:", input)

for loop

The for loop in Python can traverse any sequence of items, such as a list or a string.

The basic format of the for loop is as follows:

For variable in sequence:

loop statement

For example, use the for loop to traverse the list, the example code is as follows:

```
for result in [62,1,32]:
 print(result)
```

Output results:

62

1

32

In the above example, the for loop can display the values in the list one by one.

Considering that the range of values we use varies frequently, Python provides a built-in Range function that can generate a sequence of numbers.

The basic format of the range function in the for loop is as follows:

```
for result in range(get,set)
{
 Enter logic here
}
```

Execute loop statement

When the program executes the for loop, the loop timer variable result is set to start, and then the loop statement is executed. The result is sequentially set to all values between start and end. The loop statement is executed once for each new value set.

In an integer, the number divisible by 2 is called an even number. Now, we will develop a program to calculate the sum of even numbers between 1 and 100.

Example Calculate the Sum of Even Numbers from 1 to 100

first=0

Output=0

while i<101:

 if first%2==0:

 sum Output+=first

 first+=1

Print ("the sum of even numbers between 1 and 100 is: %s" %first")

while nesting

It just represents a nested while in a while loop.

The while nesting format is as follows:

While condition 1:

When condition 1 is met, do 1

{

while condition 2:

When condition 2 is met, do 2

}

Relevant explanations of the above formats are as follows:

(1) When the loop condition 1 is satisfied, the things to be done when the condition 1 is satisfied are executed. At this time, there may be an opportunity to execute the loop nested inside.

(2) When the cycle condition 2 is satisfied, perform the things to be done when condition 2 is satisfied until the while cycle inside is finished.

(3) When the cycle condition 2 is not satisfied, the while cycle outside the loop is finished after the execution of the things to be done by the external loop.

With this, we have completed a brief discussion about conditionals and loops in Python. We will also discuss remaining control flow statements in the further chapter. For now, in the next chapter, we will in detail discuss object-oriented programming with a lot of examples.

Chapter 12: Object oriented programming in Python

There are various forms of things in the real world, and there are various connections between these things. In a program, objects are used to map real things and the relationships between objects are used to describe the relationships between things. This idea is the object-oriented paradigm.

When we talk about object-oriented programming, we naturally think of process-oriented programming. Process-oriented programming is to analyze the steps to solve the problem, and then use functions to implement these steps one by one when using different methods.

Object-oriented programming is to decompose the problem-solving entities into multiple objects, and the purpose of establishing objects is not to complete one by one but to describe the behavior of things in the process of solving the whole problem.

The following is an example of gobang to illustrate the difference between process-oriented and object-oriented programming.

First, use the process-oriented paradigm:

1. Start the game

2. Player 1 plays first

3. Draw the picture

4. Judges the result

5. Player 2 turn

6. Draw the picture

7. Judges the result

8. Return to Step 2

9. Output Final Results

The above steps are implemented by functions respectively, and the problem is solved using a process-oriented paradigm.

Object-oriented design solves the problem from another way of thinking. When using object-oriented thinking to realize gobang, the whole gobang game can be divided into three types of objects, as follows.

1. Black and White Parties: This represents the two players

2. Chessboard system: This is responsible for drawing pictures

3. Rule system: This is responsible for judging things such as foul, winning or losing, etc.

Among the above three-class objects, the first-class object (black and white parties) is responsible for receiving the user's input and notifying the second-class object (chessboard system) to draw pieces on the chessboard, while the third-class object (rule system) judges the chessboard.

Object-oriented programming ensures the unity of functions, thus making the code easier to maintain.

For example, if we want to add the function of chess now in a process-oriented paradigm, then a series of steps of input, judgment, and display needs to be changed. Even the loops between steps need to be adjusted on a large scale, which is very troublesome.

If object-oriented development is used, only the chessboard object needs to be changed. The chessboard object saves the chessboard scores of both black and white parties, and only needs simple backtracking, without changing the display and rules. At the same time, the calling sequence of the whole object function will not change, and its changes are only partial. Thus, compared with process-oriented, object-oriented programming is more convenient for later code maintenance and function expansion.

Classes and objects

In object-oriented programming, the two most important core concepts are class and object. Objects are concrete things in real life. They can be seen and touched. For example, the book you are holding is an object.

Compared with objects, classes are abstract, which is a general designation for a group of things with the same characteristics and behaviors. For example, when I was a child, my mother said to me, "Son, you should take that kind of person as an example!" The type of people here refers to a group of people who have excellent academic results and who are polite. They have the same characteristics, so they are called "same type" people.

Relationship between Class and Object

As the saying goes, "people are grouped by category, and things are grouped by group," we collectively refer to the collection of things with similar characteristics and behaviors as categories, such as animals, airplanes, etc.

For example, the toy model can be regarded as a class and each toy as an object, thus the relationship between the toy model and the toy can be regarded as the relationship between the class and the object. Class is used to describe the common features of multiple objects and is a template for objects. An object is used to describe individuals in reality. It is an instance of a class. As can be seen, objects are created according to classes, and one class can correspond to multiple objects.

Definition of Class

In daily life, to describe a kind of category, it is necessary to explain its characteristics as well as its uses. For example, when describing such entities as human beings, it is usually necessary to give a definition or name to such things. Human characteristics include height, weight, sex, occupation, etc. Human behaviors include running, speaking, etc. The combination of human characteristics and behaviors can completely describe human beings.

The design idea of an object-oriented program is based on this design, which includes the features and behaviors of things in classes. Among them, the characteristics of things are taken as the attributes of classes, the behaviors of things are taken as the methods of classes, and objects are an instance of classes. So to create an object, you need to define a class first. The class is composed of 3 parts.

(1) Class Name: The name of the class, whose initial letter must be uppercase, such as Person.

(2) Attribute: used to describe the characteristics of things, for example, people have the characteristics of name, age, etc.

(3) Method: Used to describe the behavior of things, for example, people have behaviors such as talking and smiling.

In Python, you can use the class keyword to declare a class with the following basic syntax format:

Class {Enter the entity here}:

This is property of a class

Method of class

The following is a sample code:

class Vehicle:

attribute

Method

 def drive(self):

Print ("-drivinf Automobile--")

In the above example, the class is used to define a class named Vehicle, in which there is a drive method. As can be seen from the example, the format of the method is the same as that of the function.

The main difference is that the method must explicitly declare a self-parameter and be located at the beginning of the parameter list. Self represents the instance of the class (object) itself, which can be used to refer to the attributes and methods of the object. The specific usage of self will be introduced later with practical application.

Creating Objects from Classes

If a program wants to complete specific functions, classes alone are not enough but also instance objects need to be created according to classes.

In Python programs, you can use the following syntax to create an object:

Object {Enter the entity name here } = Class { Enter the name here} ()

For example, create an object Vehicle of driving class with the following sample code:

vehicle = driving()

In the above code, vehicle is a variable that can be used to access the properties and methods of the class. To add attributes to an object, you can use the following syntax.

Object {Enter entity here}. New {Enter attribute name} = Value

For example, use vehicle to add the color attribute to an object of driving class.

The sample code is as follows:

vehicle.color = "black"

Next, a complete case is used to demonstrate how to create objects, add attributes and call methods. Look at it and clear all your doubts.

Example Sport.py

Define Class

class Football:

kick

def kick(goal):

print ("You scored ...")

Foul

def foul(self):

print ("You cheated")

creates an object and saves its reference with the variable BMW

Barcelona = Football()

Add Attribute Representing Color

Barcelona.color = "blue"

Call Method

Barcelona.goal()

Barcelona.foul()

Access Attributes

print(Barcelona.color)

In Example, a Football class is defined, two methods kick and foul is defined in the class, then an object Barcelona of football class is created, color attribute is dynamically added and assigned to "blue", then goal () and foul () methods are called in turn, and the value of color attribute is printed out.

Structural Methods and Destructural Methods

In Python programs, two special methods are provided: __init__ () and __del__ (), which are respectively used to initialize the properties of the object and release the resources occupied by the class. This section mainly introduces these two methods in detail.

Construction method

In the previous example defining classes, we dynamically added the color attribute to the objects referenced by Barcelona. Just imagine, if you create another Football class object, you need to add attributes in the form of "object name. attribute name". For each object created, you need to add attributes once, which is very troublesome.

To solve this problem, attributes can be set when creating an object. Python provides a construction method with a fixed name of __init__ (two underscores begin and two underscores end). When creating an instance of a class, the system will automatically call the constructor to initialize the class.

To make everyone better understand, the following is a case to demonstrate how to use the construction method for initialization.

Example: uses the construction method. py

```
# Define Class
class Football:
# construction method
def __init__(kick):
Color = "blue"
# Foul
def foul(self):
print ("%s Barcelona color is " (self.color))
```

creates an object and saves its reference with the variable car

football = Football()

football.foul()

In the example, lines 4-5 re-implemented the __init__ () method, adding the color attribute to the Football class and assigning it a value of "blue", and accessing the value of the color attribute in the foul method.

No matter how many Football objects are created, the initial value of the color attribute is "blue" by default. If you want to modify the default value of the property after the object is created, you can set the value of the property by passing parameters in the construction method.

The following is a case to demonstrate how to use the construction method with parameters.

Example: uses the parametric construction method. py

Define Class

class Football:

construction method

def __init__(kick):

Color = "blue"

Foul

def foul(self):

print ("%s Barcelona color is " (self.color))

creates an object and saves its reference with the variable car

football = Football()

football.foul()

creates an object and saves its reference with the variable bmw

realmadrid = color ("white")

realmadrid.color()

In Example, lines 4 to 5 customize the construction method with parameters, and assign the value of the parameters to the color attribute, ensuring that the value of the color attribute changes with the value received by the parameters, and then still access the value of the color attribute in the toot method.

Destructor Methods

Earlier, we introduced the __init__ () method. When an object is created, the Python interpreter will call the __init__ () method by default. When deleting an object to release the resources occupied by the class, the Python interpreter calls another method by default, which is the __del__ () method.

Next, a case is used to demonstrate how to use a destructor to release the occupied resources.

example: using destructor. py

Define Class

class Football

def __init__(team, color, name):

team.name = name

team.color = color

def __del__(team):

print("--------del--------")

Realmadrid = team ("white", 1)

In Example, a class named Person is defined, the initial values of color and team are set in the __init__ () method, a print statement is added in the __del__ () method, and then an object of the Person class is created using a custom construction method.

When the program ends, the memory space it occupies will be released.

So, can we release the space manually? Yes, Del statement can be used to delete an object and release the resources it occupies.

Add the following code at the end of Example:

del realmadrid

print("---------1---------")

☐ As you can observe from the results, the program outputs "del" before "1". This is because Python has an automatic garbage collection mechanism. When the Python program ends, the Python interpreter detects whether there is currently any memory space to be freed. If there is a del statement, it will be automatically deleted; if the del statement has been manually called, it will not be automatically deleted.

With this, we have given a thorough introduction to object-oriented programming in python. In the next chapter, we will talk about control flow statements in brief. Let us go!

Chapter 13: Control flow statements in Python

Previously we have discussed Conditionals and loop statements in detail. In this chapter, we will further continue discussing control statements briefly. A lot of examples are given to make you understand the essence of the topic. Let us dive into it.

What are the control flow statements?

All conditionals, loops and extra programming logic code that executes a logical structure are known as control flow statements. We already have an extensive introduction to conditionals and loops with various examples. Now, you should remember that the control flow statements we are going to learn now are very important for program execution. They can successfully skip or terminate or proceed with logic if used correctly. We will start learning about them now with examples. Let us go!

break statement

The break statement is used to end the entire loop (the current loop body) all at once. It is preceded by a logic.

for example, the following is a normal loop:

for sample in range(10):

print("-------")

print sample

After the above loop statement is executed, the program will output integers from 0 to 9 in sequence. The program will not stop running until the loop ends. At this time, if you want the program to output only numbers from 0 to 2, you need to end the loop at the specified time (after executing the third loop statement).

Next, demonstrate the process of ending the loop with a break.

Example: break Statement

end=1

for end in range(10):

end+=1

print("-------")

if end==3:

break

print(end)

In Example, when the program goes to the third cycle because the value of the end is 3, the program will stop and print the loop until then.

continue statement

The function of continue is to end this cycle and then execute the next cycle. It will look at the logical values and continue with the process.

Next, a case is used to demonstrate the use of the continue statement below.

Example continue statement

sample=1

for sample in range(10):

sample+=1

print("-------")

if sample==3:

continue

print(sample)

In Example, when the program executes the third cycle because the value of sample is 3, the program will terminate this cycle without outputting the value of sample and immediately execute the next cycle.

Note:

(1)break/continue can only be used in a cycle, otherwise, it cannot be used alone.

(2)break/continue only works on the nearest loop in nested loops.

pass statement

Pass in Python is an empty statement, which appears to maintain the integrity of the program structure. Pass does nothing and is generally used as a placeholder.

The pass statement is used as shown in Example below.

Example pass Statement

```
for alphabet in 'University':
 if letter == 'v':
 pass
 print ('This is the statement')
 print ('Use this alphabet', letter)
print ("You can never see me again" )
```

In Example above, when the program executes pass statements because pass is an empty statement, the program will ignore the statement and execute the statements in sequence.

else statement

Earlier, when learning if statements, else statements were found outside the scope of the if conditional syntax. In fact, in addition to judgment statements, while and for loops in Python can also use else statements. When used in a loop, the else statement is executed only after the loop is completed, that is, the break statement also skips the else statement block.

Next, we will demonstrate it through a case for your better understanding of the else block.

Example: else statement

```
result = 0
```

```
while result < 5:

 print(result, " is less than 5")

 result = result + 1

else:

 print(result, " is not less than 5")
```

In Example, the else statement is executed after the while loop is terminated, that is, when the value of the result is equal to 5, the program executes the else statement.

With this, we have completed a short introduction to control flow statements in Python programming. It is always important to use control flow statements only when they are necessary. ☐ If they are used without any use case, they may start creating unnecessary blockages while programming. In the next chapter, we will give a short introduction to decision trees in Python. Let us go!

Chapter 14: Decision trees in Python

In the previous chapter, we have discussed control flow statements and now we are going to discuss a concept that is related to control flow statements. Decision trees are a logical structure that can be used to make decisions based on certain criteria. A tree is a basic data structure that is usually used to store and sort things. We will now in detail discuss decision trees in python. Let us start!

What are decision trees?

Decision trees are a programming concept in python that can be used to make decisions. They are also used to make decisions based on the inputs given. Decision trees are mostly used in machine learning to create regression and supervised algorithms. We can implement decision trees in python using the pandas library that consists of a lot of algorithms.

In the next section, we will discuss the implementation of decision trees in detail. Follow along!

Implementation of decision trees

These decision trees usually work by depending on the questions that are asked on. If the logic that is given satisfies the condition then a decision is made. If it is not satisfied then it is passed onto the other node present.

How to select?

To select a node we need to operate as described below.

if (node logic)

{ If it statisfies

then save()

else

proceed.next()

The objective of this code is that the block of statement is checked upon by various complex logical entities. After completing the check if it is not satisfied then they will skip into the next node to perform the same operation. If they satisfy the condition the position value of the tree is stored in the error for further evaluation.

Installing decision tree in python

To install or work with decision trees you need to install pandas and ski-kit learn and use dependencies to use them. You can use pip to install them.

The format is here:

pip install {Enter the platform name here}

Algorithm of the decision tree

For any data structure, it is important to follow the algorithm that has been mentioned. Now, we will in detail explain the decision tree algorithm according to the python programming language. Follow along!

Step 1:

At first, you need to consider all the data that is present as a root set.

Step 2:

In the next step, you need to understand the attributes that are present and should need to work on parameters to display the results.

Step 3:

In this step, you need to perform recursive operations on the values that you have used for the comparison.

Step 4:

In the last step, you need to use different statistical and pseudo methods to understand the node calculations.

Data import for decision trees

To import data that works on decision trees you need to use pandas third-party library. You can either fetch the URL details or you can use CSV format to send information. You can even use the import statement to get the task done.

Data slicing for decision trees

It is often hard to send a lot of information to the decision tree at once. To counter this problem python provides data slicing operations where the data can be divided according to your requirement.

To perform excellent decision tree operations, it is important to master complex computer science topics such as the Gini Index, Entropy which are out of the scope of this book. If you are interested to construct your own decision tree algorithms, we recommend you to learn in-depth about the Information gain mechanism.

With this, we have completed a brief explanation about decision trees in Python. In the next chapter, we will learn about exception handling in detail. Let us go!

Chapter 15: Essential programming in Python

In python, it is essential to deal with errors to make programs run. Whenever a python program stops running for the user due to warnings and errors it is advised to show the reasons for the end-user. Python programmers should develop this skill by understanding the essence of exception handling in python. It is very essential for making things work smoothly. In this chapter, we will discuss this in detail with examples. Let us start!

Brief Introduction of Anomalies

In Python, errors generated during the execution of a program are called exceptions, such as list indexes crossing boundaries, opening files that do not exist, etc.

For example, an error occurs when running the following program code.

open(data.txt)

FileNotFound { There is no such file: 'data.txt' }

Abnormal Class

In Python, all Exception classes are subclasses of Exception. The exceptions class is defined in the Exceptions module, which is in Python's built-in namespace and can be used directly without import.

In the previous chapters, the program threw an exception every time it encountered an error in executing the program. If the exception object is not processed and captured, the program will terminate execution with a traceback, which includes the name of the error (such as NameError), the reason and the line number where the error occurred.

Here are some common exceptions.

1.NameError

Attempting to access an undeclared variable raises a NameError.

For example:

print(dude)

The error message is as follows:

NameError: There is no such namespace

The above information indicates that the interpreter did not find foo in any namespace.

2.ZeroDivisionError

When the divisor is zero, a ZeroDivisionError exception is thrown.

For example:

1/0

The error message is as follows:

ZeroDivisionError: division by zero is not possible

Any numerical value divided by zero will lead to the above exception.

3.SyntaxError

When the interpreter finds a SyntaxError, it will throw a syntax error exception.

For example:

list = ["two","four","six"]

for result in list

 print(result)

In the above example, due to the lack of a colon after the for loop, the program has the following error message:

SyntaxError: This is not the correct syntax

The SyntaxError exception is the only exception that does not occur at runtime. It represents an incorrect structure in Python code that prevents the program from executing. These errors generally occur at compile-time, and the interpreter cannot convert the script into byte code.

4.IndexError

An IndexError exception is thrown when using an index that does not exist in the sequence.

For example:

example = []

example[0]

In the above example, there is no element in the list. When accessing the first element of the list with index 0, the following error message appears:

IndexError: There is no such index

The above information indicates that the index value of the list is beyond the range of the list.

5.KeyError

When using a key that does not exist in the map, a KeyError exception is thrown.

For example:

Thisresult = {'number':'explain','port':7232}

Thisresult['interpret']

In the above example, there are only two keys host and port in myDict dictionary. When obtaining the corresponding value of the interpret key, the following error message appears:

KeyError: 'interpret'

The above information indicates that there is a key server that does not exist in the dictionary.

6.FileNotFoundError

When trying to open a file that does not exist, a file not found IOError exception is thrown.

For example:

second = open("test")

In the above example, using the open method to open a file or directory named test, the following error message appears:

FileNotFoundError: { There is nothing that exists with this name}

The above information indicates that no file or directory named test was found.

7.AttributeError

An AttributeError exception is thrown when attempting to access an unknown object attribute.

For example:

class Aeroplane(object):

fly

```
flight = Aeroplane()
Aeroplane.color = "white"
```

In the above example, the Aeroplane class does not define any attributes and methods. After creating an instance of the Aeroplane class, the color attribute is dynamically added to the instance referenced by the flight, and then the following error message appears when accessing it's color and name attributes:

AttributeError: 'Aeroplane' object has no attribute 'value'

The above information indicates that the color attribute is defined in the Aeroplane instance, so it can be accessed by flight.color. However, the name attribute is not defined, so an error occurs when accessing the name attribute.

In the next section, we will discuss exception handling in detail. Follow along!

Exception handling

Python's ability to handle exceptions is very powerful. It can accurately feedback error information and help developers to accurately locate the location and cause of problems. Try-except statements are used in Python to handle exceptions. Among them, try statements are used to detect exceptions and exception statements are used to catch exceptions.

Capture Simple Exceptions

The try-except statement defines a piece of code to monitor exceptions and provides a mechanism to handle exceptions.

The simplest try-except statement format is as follows:

```
try :
# Here is the place where logic goes
```

except :

Here we enter the error details

When an error occurs in a statement in a try block, the program will no longer continue to execute the statement in the try block, but will directly execute the statement that handles the exception in exception.

To make readers better understand, the following is a case to demonstrate how to use a simple try-except statement to try to capture the possible exceptions caused by dividing two numbers, as shown in the example.

Example: Simple Exceptions. py

```
try:
print("-"*64)
first = input ("You should enter the first entity")
second = input ("You should enter the second entity")
print(int(first)/int(second))
print("-"*64)
except ZeroDivisionError:
print ("Number 64 cannot be divided")
```

In Example, two values input by the user are received in the input function of the try clause, wherein the first value is taken as the dividend and the other value is taken as the divisor. If the divisor is 0, the program will throw a ZeroDivisionError exception. In this case, the exception clause will catch the exception and print the exception information.

Run the program and enter the first number of 64 and the second number of 5 in the console. The result will be shown. By analyzing this carefully you will understand how exception handling works.

From the results, it can be seen that when the program is abnormal, the program will not be terminated again, but the user will be reminded according to the message set by himself. Note that as long as errors are monitored, the program will execute the statements except and will no longer execute the unexecuted statements in a try.

Capture the description information of the anomaly

Multiple exceptions can be caught through an except clause. The two errors of Example are combined into an except clause as follows.

try:

 first = input ("Enter the first entity")

 second = input ("Enter the second entity")

 print(int(first)/int(second))

except (ZeroDivisionError, Enter the value here):

 print ("Get a value")

At this time, no matter anyone of the above two exceptions occurs, the statement inside the exception will be printed. However, printing only one error message is not helpful. To distinguish different error information, as can be used to obtain error information fed back by the system.

Capture all abnormalities

Even if the program can handle multiple exceptions, it is impossible to prevent them, and, likely, some exceptions are still not caught. In Example, if num1 is written as nmn1 when writing the program, an error message similar to the following will be obtained.

NameError: name 'nmn1' is not defined

In such a case, the SyntaxError exception can be captured on the original basis. If there are dozens of errors in the program, it is very troublesome to catch these exceptions. To solve this situation, the exception clause can not specify the exception type, so it can handle any type of exception.

To make readers understand better, the function of capturing all abnormalities is added as an example here.

Example: Captures All Exceptions

```
# captures all exceptions
try:
first = input ("Use this as first entity")
second = input ("Use this as second entity")
print(int(first)/int(second))
except :
print ("You got this error")
```

In Example, the except statement does not indicate the type of exception, and all possible errors of the program are uniformly handled in the statement.

As can be seen from the results of the two runs, the prompt information for all exceptions is the same. Another way to catch all Exceptions is to use the exception class after the exception statement. Since the Exception class is the parent of all exception classes, all exceptions can be caught.

No exception was caught

In the if statement, when all the conditions are not met, the else statement is executed. Similarly, if the try statement does not capture any error information, it will not execute any exception statement but will execute the else statement.

To make readers understand better, we add else statement based on the above example.

Example else statement. py

```
try:
first = input ("Use this as first entity")
second = input ("Use this as second entity")
print(int(first)/int(second))
except :
print ("You got this error")
else:
```

print ("The program runs normally and no exception is caught")

In Example, when an error is detected in the try statement, the printing statement in except will be executed and the description information of the exception will be output. When there is no error, the print statement in else will be executed.

With this, we have completed a brief explanation of essential programming concepts. In the next chapter, we will discuss file management in detail. Follow along!

Chapter 16: File management in Python

Python is a programming language that deals with a lot of file operations in general. It has a special library to deal with file management functionalities. This chapter is a comprehensive introduction to all of the file management methods that are available in python. We also provided python programming code statements for your further analysis. Let us start!

Opening and Closing of Files

Let's imagine, if you want to use a word document to write a resume, what should be the process?

(1) Open Word document software and create a new file.

(2) Write personal resume information.

(3) save the file.

(4) Close Word document software.

Similarly, the overall process of manipulating files in Python is very similar to the process of writing a resume using Word.

(1) Open a file or create a new one.

(2) Read/write data.

(3) close the file.

Next, we will introduce the opening and closing of files respectively.

Opening of Files

In Python, the open method is used to open a file in the following syntax format:

Open (Name of the file [access mode information])

In the above format, the filename must be filled in, and information about access mode is optional (access mode will be described in detail later in this chapter).

For example, open a file named "country.txt" with the following sample code:

entity = open('country.txt')

It should be noted that if the access mode is not specified when opening the file by using the open method, the file must be guaranteed to exist, otherwise, the following abnormal information will be reported.

FileNotFound { // We are unable to find the file specified}

Document Mode

If you use the open method to open a file with only one file name, then we can only read one file. If the open file allows writing data, the mode of the file must be indicated. There are many access modes for files in Python.

"RB", "WB" and "AB" modes all operate files in binary mode. Usually, these modes are used to process files of binary types, such as sound or image.

Closing of Documents

Always use the close method to close open files. Even if a file will be automatically closed after the program exits, considering the safety of the data, the close method should be used to close the file after each use of the file. Otherwise, once the program crashes, the data in the file may not be saved.

The close method is very simple to use, with specific examples as follows:

Create a new file with the file name country.txt

sample = open('country.txt', 'w')

Close this file

sample.close()

Reading and writing of documents

The most important ability of a file is to receive data or provide data. The reading and writing of files is nothing more than writing data into or reading data from files. Next, this section will explain the reading and writing of files respectively.

Writing Documents

Writing data to a file needs to be completed by using the write method. when operating a file, every time the write method is called, the written data will be appended to the end of the file.

Example: Writing Data to Files

f = open('data.txt', 'w')

f.write('This is an example for writing data')

f.close()

After the program runs, a file named data.txt will be generated under the path where the program is located. Open the file and you can see that the data was successfully written.

Note:

When writing data to a file, if the file does not exist, the system will automatically create a file and write the data. If the file exists, the data of the original file will be emptied and the new data will be rewritten.

Reading documents

When reading data from a file, it can be obtained in a variety of ways, as follows.

1. Use the read method to read the file

The read method can read data from a file, and its definition syntax is as follows:

read(size)

In the above method, the size represents the length of data to be read from the file, in bytes. If the size is not specified, then all data of the file is read.

Example: Use read Method to Read Files

example = open('data.txt', 'r')

value = f.read(22)

value = f.read()

2. Use the readlines method to read files

If the content of the file is very small, you can use the readlines method to read the content of the entire file at one time. The readlines method returns a list with each element in the list being each row of data in the file. Suppose the file "data. txt" contains three lines of data then the way to read the file using the readlines method is shown in the example below.

Example: Use the readlines Method to Read Files

sample = open('data.txt', 'r') 2 entity = f.readlines()

□ *Application of File Reading and Writing-Making Backup of Files*

In actual development, the reading and writing of files can accomplish many functions. For example, the back up of files is the process of reading and writing files.

□ At this time, if you want to make a backup file of data.txt, you need to read the data of the original file and write the acquired data into the backup file. Compared with the original file, the backup file stores the same data as the original file.

Example: Making a Backup of Files

secondfile = firstfile [result]+'[copy]'+data]

secondfile= open(secondfilename, 'w')

for instance in firstfile.readlines():

secondfile.write(lineContent)

Positioning, Reading, and Writing of Files

In the previous study, the reading and writing of documents were all done in sequence. However, in actual development, it may be necessary to start reading and writing from a specific location of the file. At this time, we need to locate the reading and writing location of the file, including obtaining the current reading and writing location of the file and locating the specified reading and writing location of the file.

In the next section, the two positioning methods are introduced in detail as follows.

1. Use the tell method to obtain the current read-write location of the file

In the process of reading and writing files, if you want to know the current location, you can use the tell method to get it. The tell method returns the current location of the file, that is, the current location of the file pointer.

Example: Use tell Method to Obtain the Current Read and Write Location of Files

place = get.tell()

print ("Required position:", place ")

value = set.read(3)

print ("The data read is:", str ")

Find Position of the page

place = find.tell()

2. Use the seek method to locate the specified read-write location of the file

If it is necessary during the process of reading and writing files to start reading and writing from the specified location, you can use the seek method.

The syntax for defining the seek method is as follows:

seek(offset[whence])

The parameters of the seek method are described below.

(1)offset: Indicates the offset, that is, the number of bytes to be moved.

(2)whence indicates the direction.

There are three values for this parameter:

(1) The default value of Seek _ Set or 0: Whence parameter indicates offset from the starting position of the file.

(2) seek _ cur or 1: indicates offset from the current position of the file

(3) seek _ end or 2: offset from the end of the file.

Example: Use the seek method to locate the specified location of the file

value.seek(4)

Find Current position

place=get.tell()

print ("the current file location is:", position ")

Renaming and Deleting Files

Sometimes, files need to be renamed and deleted. Python's os module already includes these functions by default.

Next, this section will explain the renaming and deletion of files in detail.

Renaming of Files

The rename method of the os module can complete the renaming of files in the following format:

os.rename(Nameofthesource,dst)

In the above format, src refers to the file name to be modified, dst refers to the modified new file name.

For example, the example code for renaming the file "Hotel. txt" to "Restaurant" is as follows:

import os

Os.rename ("hotel. txt", "restaurant. txt")

Deletion of documents

The remove method of the os module can complete the deletion of files in the following format:

os.remove(path)

In the above format, path refers to the file under the specified path.

For example, the example code for deleting the file "Tour. txt" under the current path is as follows:

import os

os.remove ("tour. txt")

Folder operations

In the actual development, it is sometimes necessary to operate the folder in a program way, such as creating and deleting. Just as the os module is required for file operation, the os module is also required for folder operation. In the next section, the creation of the folder, the acquisition of the current directory, the change of the default directory of the file and the deletion of the folder will be explained as follows.

1. Create a folder

The mkdir method of the os module is used to create folders, and the example code is as follows:

import os

Os.mkdir ("Executive")

2. Get the current directory

The getcwd method of os module is used to obtain the current directory.

The sample code is as follows:

138

import os

os.{Get the current directory}()

3. Change the default directory

The chdir method of the os module is used to change the default directory, for example, the code for changing the current directory to the directory at the next higher level is as follows:

import os

os.chdir("../")

4. Get the directory list

The listdir method of os module is used to obtain the directory list. For example, to obtain the subdirectory list under the current path, the code is as follows:

import os

os.listdir("./")

5. Delete the folder

The rmdir method of the os module is used to delete folders. For example, the following code deletes the "Executive" directory under the current path:

import os

Os.rmdir ("Executive")

With this, we have completed a brief and detailed explanation to the file management system in Python. With this, we have completed a deep journey into the Python universe. Now, it's time for you to implement these concepts in real-world programming. All the best!

Conclusion

Glad that you have reached the end of this book. I hope you have enjoyed the content provided in the book as much we loved making this book.

What to do next?

As you have completed a complex and thorough book that deals with Python programming it is now a huge test for you to apply your programming skills on real time projects. There are a lot of open-source projects that are waiting for a contribution. Remember that reading a lot of Python code will also help you understand the programming logics that python possesses.

That's it! Thanks for purchasing this book again and All the best!

PYTHON FOR INTERMEDIATE

A practical guide for intermediate using of Python

Will Norton

Introduction

Machine learning is one of the most fast-developing computer technologies in this decade and is estimated to occupy the mainstream industry by 2025.

A lot of industries are developing applications and algorithms to use machine learning functionalities. For example, Google is developing a machine-learning algorithm to verify the search results quality.

We can implement machine learning functionalities using different languages such as Python, R, and Java.

However, Python is said to give excellent results from the data scientist's perspective. In the previous book of this module, we have discussed Python programming language. This book explains advanced Python concepts from a data scientist perspective.

A lot of the topics we will discuss will give a clear understanding of its importance in the machine learning environment.

Why we wrote this book?

There are fewer resources that provide valuable knowledge related to Python that is required for improving machine learning skills.

We wrote a book that can help beginners to grasp the complex python topics to use them in implementing machine learning algorithms.

Python has a lot of third-party libraries that can help a data scientist to improve his technical ability.

However, to use these third-party libraries it is essential to master advanced Python programming. For this sole reason, we have written a book that lets you understand various Python topics easily.

How to use this book?

This book is a comprehensive guide to Python and also comprises various programming examples.

We recommend you to install Python in your system and work with the Python code to look at the results. Dealing with errors all by yourselves will help you understand the essence of the programming language.

There are a lot of books that can help you master the Python programming, but there are only a few books that will help you think like a programmer.

This book is one of them. All the best and have a happy learning experience. Let us go!

Chapter 1: What is Python? Why Python?

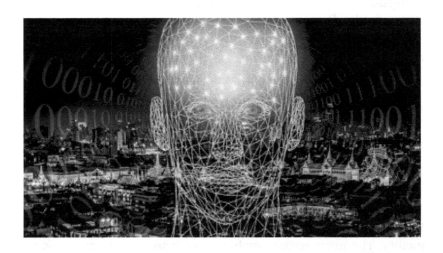

Python is a programming language that has been declared as one of the easiest programming languages to learn for beginners.

Apart from its simple syntax and intuitive functionalities, the availability of abundant resources is also a reason for Python's success among the masses.

Python is the most popular language in GitHub and comprises thousands of open source projects and third-party libraries that can help you create complex software.

Python is also a recommended language to learn for enthusiastic data scientists.

Machine learning, a famous computer science branch relies on Python libraries to analyze the data. In this book, we will look at Python functionalities from a machine learning perspective. In the next section, we will discuss Python functionalities with good, valid technical information.

Why Python is famous?

There are over 100 programming languages available for computer programmers and computer scientists nowadays. Out of all, Python has occupied a prominent position because of its active community which is always trying to clear off the bugs and update with new features.

A study proposed why Python is famous among programmers. We will in this section discuss some of those reasons that made Python a programmer's favorite.

Here are the valid reasons:

1) Quality

When you create programs with Python, they are often of high quality. The users encounter fewer bugs and it is easy to update the programs using different Python modules.

Python supports various programming paradigms such as procedural and object-oriented programming to reuse the code effectively. It is also easily readable because of indentation techniques. This high quality in the programming syntax had made programmers fell in love with it.

2) Productivity

Other programming languages such as Java and C are statistically typed languages and require a huge amount of code to even process very fewer data.

Python simplifies the code to be written and requires only half of the programming code when compared to the other languages. This increases productivity and can adversely increase the quality of applications that are being developed.

3) Portability

Unlike Java, which runs its applications only when a JVM is present Python can run software applications on any platform. All you need to do is to add a few lines of code that will process the software to run on other platforms.

Python applications can also be deployed to run in web and database environments with a slight change in code. All these portable advantages make developers use Python as a primary language when developing cross-platform applications.

4) Third-party Libraries

Python has a lot of default functions in the standard library. There are mathematical and statistical functions that can be used in developing data science applications.

However, standard library functions are often not sufficient to develop complex software. Here comes the concept of third-party libraries which can be easily imported to a Python project. With the help of third-party libraries, you can develop complex and advanced software using Python.

5) Enjoyment

As simple and intuitive it is, Python's success also depends on its level of enjoyment to the developers. It is easy to maintain and comprises fewer hiccups than the other programming languages. Python has various modules that can automate tasks. All these advantages bind up to make Python an entertaining programming language for the developers.

Because of the above technical reasons, Python has become famous among the programming community and has expanded its user base. In the next section, we will describe some Python applications in day-to-day life.

Applications of Python

Python is used by approximately 1.5 million developers according to the statistics. A lot of websites, APIs, software are developed using Python as a primary language.

This success of Python is also because of its open-source nature that lets programmers use the language as they like. This is the reason why Python is also used as a scripting language by many hackers.

However, it is not evident to call Python as a scripting language on this remark. We consider Python as a multi-use language that can be useful for many fields and users.

Here are some multi-national companies that use Python for their products:

a) Google extensively uses Python to build and update its search engine crawlers.

b) YouTube was initially written on Python. A lot of YouTube integration services still use Python.

c) A lot of Netflix recommendation algorithms use Python to resource them effectively.

d) Dropbox, a famous storage service uses Python to encrypt the files.

Apart from these few examples, Python is also used in iRobot to develop Robots.

Here are some technical fields where Python is extensively used:

a) Systems programming

This is a branch of computer science where we can develop system management tools such as compilers, interpreters and shell tools that can interact with the system at the kernel level. Python is very adaptable to this branch of computer science as it has several extensible libraries that can help to create effective programs.

b) Internet

Python is an easy language to create small internet scripts. A lot of script kiddies use programs developed using Python to crack account passwords. A lot of brute forcing tools also use Python to automate dictionary attacks on an authenticated server.

Python is also famous for developing web applications that can store sensitive information. A lot of WebCrawler and web analysis services use Python to curate the information.

c) Integration systems

A lot of hardware components such as Arduino works effectively only when they are programmed to do. Usually, embedded systems work well with traditional structural languages such as C and C++.

Python has a lot of libraries that can help to integrate already written python code to embedded systems.

d) Database programming

Databases are an essential entity to store and manipulate information. There are a lot of database query languages to store and query data. However, Python is used by many database administrators to constantly monitor the intrusion detection system that is available.

There are a lot of Python libraries that can help developers to automatically check for viruses and store a backup in the remote server.

e) Machine Learning

Machine learning is a booming computer science field where we can analyze the information and data that is present. Python has a lot of libraries such as SciPy and Pandas to maintain the data in a significant way.

This book will list out various Python features to become good at machine learning.

Apart from these fields, Python is also used by hackers, malware reverse engineers, and Computer scientists to do various analytic experiments.

In the next section, we will discuss the advantage of Python over various other languages that are available.

Let us go!

What are Python's strengths?

Python is suggested for beginners by experienced programmers because it helps you to understand all the basics that every programming language use.

Python is usually a combined mixup of all the programming paradigms that are used. We will give you a clear understanding of this below.

a) Supports both functional and object-oriented

Python, unlike Java and C++, uses functional programming along with the object-oriented paradigm. This gives a scope to learn both technologies as a beginner.

A lot of core concepts such as polymorphism, inheritance, and functions will be covered while learning Python.

b) Open-source

Python is developed by enthusiast contributors from all around the world. It is free to create programs and distribute them.

This open-source nature gives programmers to experiment with the code and create some innovative applications.

c) Powerful

It is powerful when compared with other popular programming languages. It supports dynamic typing and is unnecessary to declare the variable and list sizes before compiling the program.

Python uses a garbage mechanism and sends all the useless system variables to dump. This improves the performance of the program in an exponential manner.

d) Default tools

Python offers a lot of very useful system tools. It can perform a lot of string operations easily using these default tools. It is also important to understand these modules to perform operations in a better way using Python.

e) Easy to use

Unlike traditional programming languages such as C and C++ Python is easy to use. C and C++ offer different paradigms that can confuse developers to operate. Python uses less indentation and it is easy to maintain the code. Python also is better than Java because it is not a statically typed language. In java, you need to introduce different useless variables to maintain the flow of the program structure. However, in Python, you use only what you need. This is one of the reasons Python is considered a better language for developing Machine Learning applications.

How to learn Python?

Python has a generous community that shares a lot of resources and sample projects to encourage beginners to understand the importance and beauty of Python.

This book is also a genuine approach to help you understand all the moderate level topics of Python to implement in developing Artificial intelligence and data science applications.

We suggest you to look at an open-source project and understand the essence of the logic by the constant implementation of the topics you have learned in this book.

That's it.

In this chapter, we have got a thorough introduction to the importance of Python from various sections.

Hope this chapter gave you a sufficient introduction to help you get hooked up with the topic. I

n the next chapter of this book, we will discuss different ways to install Python in the system.

Let us go!

Chapter 2: How to install python on your PC?

In the previous chapter, we have discussed the importance of Python along with its important features. In this chapter, we will discuss installing

Python in various operating systems. We will also discuss installing third party modules in Python using various package managers.

Let us start!

Checking Python Version

Usually, in Linux and Mac ox operating systems, Python is installed by default. However, it is recommended to check the version of Python using the command prompt.

Windows users need to download the installation package from the Python website.

How to check the Python version?

Open terminal or command prompt depending on your system to check whether Python is installed.

Always try to open the terminal using the administrator privileges for accurate results.

Enter the following formats:

python

python 2

python 3

If Python is installed on the system, you will get a result that displays the version of the Python that is installed.

It will also provide various options that can be very useful for beginners to understand popular commands for managing Python programs.

However, if there are no traces of the Python installation folder in the system then the terminal will return an error. Please check with the above commands in your operating system, and if your terminal sends a command error, then it is time to install the Python using the below guide.

Follow along!

How to install Python in windows?

Step 1:

First, it is important to choose the version you are willing to install in your system. We recommend you to look at the next chapter to understand about different available Python versions.

You can also look at Python online documentation to choose the suitable python version according to your requirements.

Step 2:

After selecting the python version, visit the official website to download the Python version. You need to select a 32 or 64-bit option to download the version that will be installed with no errors.

You can either download a .msi package or a .exe application according to your wish. After downloading the installation file, all you need to do is open the file with administrator privileges.

Step 3:

After we start the installation, you will get an interface that asks to enter the directory to install Python.

You can either install Python with the default directory or can change the directory according to your requirements.

Note: Make sure that there are no spaces in the directory names as sometimes Python installation will give an error.

Step 4:

At the last step of the installation, you need to update the environment variable so that Python will run on the command prompt on the system. Once the installation is finished you can crosscheck whether the installation is successful using the procedure explained before.

With this, we have learned about installing a basic Python package in the system.

In the next section, we will discuss various Python modules necessary for developing complex Python programs.

What are the other alternatives?

Python users should remember that there are several replica interpreters of Python that can be installed on the windows system.

Some are CPython, Pypy which are famous for their customization abilities.

However, we recommend you to try the original Python versions for advanced usage abilities and faster processing.

How to install Python in Mac OS?

Mac operating system has a default Python 2.x version already installed on the Python operating system. Mac operating system uses Python to control various system operations.

However, if you are keen on updating your Python version for developing programs follow the below section.

Step 1:

In the first step, you need to visit the Python official download page. The website will automatically determine your system configuration and will list you a .dmg package installer to download.

Thoroughly check the version name before you are downloading.

Step 2:

After clicking on the .dmg package installer you will be asked to enter your operating system authentication detail for security reasons.

The installer will also ask you about the default directory location.

Step 3:

In the next step, you need to enter the customization options. You can also use the automatic option to let the installer give the best results according to your system configuration. After it finishes the installation it is recommended to reboot the system and check the Python version using the terminal as mentioned in the previous sections.

Are you not interested in the Terminal operation?

Usually, Python programs are compiled in the command line interpreter or terminal. Normally, Programmers need to save a python script using a text editor and compile it from the terminal.

However, a lot of the developers are not comfortable dealing with command-line operations.

For programmers who are more inclined towards graphical user interfaces, Python provides a GUI package to install on the system.

This package is known as the Tkinter application and can be downloaded from the Python official website.

After installing can also add add-ons to customize your graphical interface.

Installing/Upgrading Python in Linux

Linux is an operating system that is used by most of the programmers and technical enthusiasts to perform tasks and to develop programs. Linux, unlike Windows and Mac, relies mostly on command line operations.

Usually, python is pre-installed in a lot of Linux distros.

If you are unaware, you can just check the Python version and proceed with the further installation process as given below.

Step 1:

You can download the Python .deb package from the Python's official website. You can use sudo operations to install the package in your system.

If you are not technically sound enough to install using the sudo operation, you can also use package managers such as RPM to install the python package.

Step 2:

After installing the package all you need to do is enter python on the terminal and look for the obtained results. You can also upgrade Python to the newer versions by changing the build script present in the Python installation folder.

In Linux, you may face conflicts while using two different versions of Python in the same system.

So, always make sure you have uninstalled the previous Python versions from the system.

Using REPL

REPL is the most basic Python component necessary to run arithmetic operations.

This component is responsible to input the values and output results. It is like a lexical analysis tool for Python. You can use REPL mode to check whether or not python is installed.

Here are some operations you can perform to confirm the Python installation in the system:

a) Do arithmetic operations

Run the following commands on your command line:

>>> 4747+3737

>>> 3424*242

>>> 63634/27

If you are getting results with no errors, then Python is successfully installed in the system.

b) Assigning variables

Variables are an entity that can store values and repeat them whenever we need it.

Here is an example:

>>> r = 446

Now try to print the assigned variable

>>> r

If you get 446 as the result then you can confirm that Python is successfully installed in your system.

Learning about Help command

Python provides a help command that will inform you about various operations that the interpreter can perform.

You can also check the online documentation to know more about the system functions and libraries.

Here is the format:

>>> help

By using this command, you can print out all the function prompts in order. Help () function can understand details about different system functions.

Every IDE also comprises a help folder that can be used to regulate information.

Using pip

Python is a programming language that uses modules and packages to develop an efficient program.

A lot of modules need to be downloaded from websites such as GitHub into the system.

To make this procedure easy, Python has developed a PyPI index that lists out all the eligible python modules.

Learning how to use pip is an essential skill for programmers. Pip can be installed using the Sudo commands.

Before trying to install a module using pip, we suggest you look at the Python module index.

After you enter the module name, the pip search module will start batch searching the module from different resources. If it finds the module, then using the downloading module it will install on your preferred directory.

Here is the command:

sudo pip install {enter the package name here}

Pip can be used in all the operating systems available.

All you need to have is a supported Python version in the system.

Using easy_install

easy_install is another alternative to pip to install different modules directly into the system.

With easy_install you can directly change the setup script to automatically make changes to the package being downloaded.

However, unlike pip, it is not simple and needs advanced learning capabilities to master it.

We recommend you to look at easy_install documentation to learn more about it.

Other IDE's to download

In this chapter, we discussed the default Python interpreter that Python comes with.

It is often recommended for beginners to make things look simpler instead of confusing them with different functionalities.

However, if you are interested, you can check out different IDE's that can develop Python programs.

We recommend Pycharm IDE to understand the different complex functionalities of Python.

Pycharm IDE also offers various debugging features to make the development of programs easy.

How to run a Python script?

After installing every necessary component, it is now time to know how to run a python script in the command line environment.

Step 1:

First, open a text editor of your choice and create a file with extension .py. In this text file enter the script and save it in your desired folder.

Step 2:

Now start the Python interpreter using Python command in the terminal. After entering the Python instance, you need to enter the following command to run the program.

>>> python filename.py

If there are no errors in the program, your file will run according to your requirements.

However, if there are any runtime errors and warning your program will be halted and it will display the results.

With this, we have completed a brief introduction to installing Python in different operating systems.

It is important to use this chapter as a reference to install different modules that will be introduced in the next chapters in this book.

In the next chapter, we will discuss different Python versions. As said before, it is important to choose the best version according to your needs.

Let us go!

Chapter 3: Different Versions of Python?

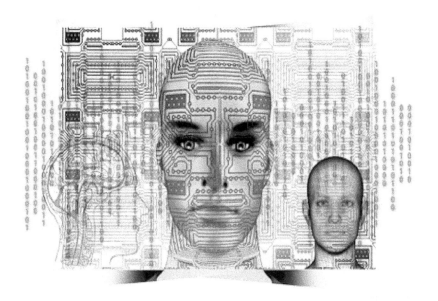

Python is a programming language that has been constantly developed by various programmers individually by collaborating with different resources.

In 1984, python's first version was released and for years it has been constantly updated with various functionalities.

In this chapter, we will discuss various Python versions and their abilities.

Let us go!

Which version most programmers use?

As of this writing, Python programmers largely rely upon Python 2.x versions for developing applications. Even after 10 years of their release, Python 3.x versions are not widely used by the community for its complex implementation of the functions.

However, Python 3.x versions also provide a lot of new features for advanced machine learning applications.

As this book focuses on Machine learning, we recommend you to try Python 3.x versions to develop applications.

Why are versions important?

When a programming language is developed there is often scope for bugs and security issues that can destroy the reputation.

This is one reason programming languages are often updated to newer versions with better compatibility.

Python developers in 2008 have started providing a 3.x version of Python with advanced functionalities, but with a change in syntax and implementation format.

Programmers are already comfortable with the 2.x version functionalities and did not go along with the flow.

However, as years passed Python 3.x has improved drastically and is now an efficient version of Python with advanced features.

The Python downloads homepage provides all these versions to download at a click.

All you need to do is understand and analyze which software version fits your needs. In the next section, we will provide complete features of all the major Python versions that got released.

Let us go!

History of Python versions

a) Python version 1

The first version of Python is developed and released in 1984. At that time, C is a popular language and is holding a good percentage of the programming market. By 1995, the python developers have included higher-order functions such as lambda and maps in the package.

The first version of Python is a huge success when looked at from a programming perspective. However, it is still not a programmer's favorite due to different compatibility reasons.

b) Python version 2

Python version 2 has changed the impact of Python in the programming world. A lot of new features such as list comprehensions and functional programming are introduced in this version of Python. Also, version 2 has made python function declaration much easier.

A lot of new concepts such as garbage mechanism and operator overloading are introduced to make this version easier to operate and maintain.

Till 2020, Python developers will maintain the version 2 python.

c) Python version 3

Python version 3 didn't do well in the programming arena when it is first introduced. A lot of programmers complained about the function declarations when it is first released.

However, as time passed with updated versions Python has shown its impact in the programming world.

A lot of advanced scientific applications started to use system functions introduced in Python 3 to implement their programs.

Python 3 also made a lot of changes to type declarations and has moved on to become one of the most successful versions of Python.

Which Python version you should choose?

It is a programmer choice to pick up the version he is more comfortable with. However, here is a suggestion that experienced programmers give to the beginners.

" Always chose the version of the Python according to your requirements.

If you want to develop a simple crawler application then it makes sense to use an older version.

If you are trying to build an advanced application that involves various new functionalities, we recommend you to try the newer versions"

Which version is best for Data scientists?

In this book, we mostly discuss Python version 3. This version is more supportive of machine learning libraries and consists of a lot of list operations.

As we deal with a huge chunk of data manipulating list items is a mandatory task. So, we recommend you to try Python version 3 to develop machine learning projects.

Which version is the most popular?

As of now, a lot of web and mobile applications are being developed using Python version 2. However, after 2020 Python will officially stop supporting Python 2 and evidentially after that, we will see a bounce in the number of programmers using Python 3.

According to a recent study conducted by Harvard University, Python 2 is one of the simplest and intuitive Python versions that ever got released.

With this, we have completed a brief introduction to Python versions in this chapter.

In the next chapter, we will discuss functional programming in detail.

Follow along!

Chapter 4: Functional Programming and Comprehension

Functions are a mathematical concept that can be used to repeat the tasks in a definite manner.

Traditional programming languages adopted this in programming to automate repetitive tasks.

However, with time developers started deploying various system functions to make programming languages more intuitive and operative.

In this chapter, we will in detail discuss various functionalities that functional programming offers with a lot of examples.

Follow along!

Characteristics of Functional programming

Functional programming contrary to the belief can cooperate with both imperative and object-oriented paradigms.

Here are some of the objectives to remember to reconsider whether a programming language supports a complete functional paradigm or not.

1) Functions are also objects. They can be used to perform every single task that objects can perform. They can be used to call a function from within a function.

2) A lot of functional programming paradigms use recursions to loop the structures. Some functional programming paradigms only offer recursion for looping the tasks.

3) Functional programming also works with lists. They are often used to process and loop through the lists.

4) Functional programming is not very comfortable in dealing with statements. However, they can be used very effectively to evaluate the expressions that hold a logical entity.

5) Functional programming also offers higher-order functions with exact precision.

Python follows all the characteristics mentioned above and is called a pure functional language. In the next section, we will in detail discuss using functions in Python.

Let us go!

What are functions?

Functions are a reusable code segment that can be used to repeat the tasks all at a time according to the specified needs.

For example, Look at the following pattern:

'{}'

'{}{}'

'{}{}{}'

For our requirement, we need to display 100 of these pairs in a straight line. You can use the print function to display the result after a lot of hard work.

However, this method is not feasible and is not preferred by programmers.

Here, functions can be used to assign the pattern and call them how many times we need and wherever we need.

You can use a looping statement to loop the pattern 100 times.

In the next section, we will achieve this result using functions in Python.

Follow along!

How to define a function?

The function should be defined according to certain regular specifications that Python language possesses.

Here is the format that functions use in Python

def {Enter name of the function} [Enter the parameters here]

Here is an example:

def sum(a,b)

After defining a function all you need to do is create a step by step logical expression for the body of the function.

How to call a function?

After defining a function, you need to know the procedure to call it whenever you need it.

Function calls can be achieved in Python by using the following format:

Nameofthefunction ()

Exercise 1: Print 100 lines of the '{}' pattern using a function

Here is the Python code:

```
def funpattern()
{
   for (i=100;i++)
   {
      print ( " {}")
      i++;
   }
}
Print( " Here is the result")
funpattern()
```

Function parameters

Parameters are necessary for functions to define default values. Variables are usually pointed out to parameters in the function and are necessary for logical execution.

There are usually default parameters that define the essence of the function.

Here is the format:

[Function parameter 1, Function parameter 2 ...... Function parameter n]

It is important to remember that the function parameter can be a dynamic number.

You can usually use these parameters to return values. In the next section, we will give an example that will help you understand recursion in detail.

Follow along!

What is recursion?

Recursion is a mathematical phenomenon where a function calls itself until the condition is satisfied. Recursion can decrease the code length of the program very effectively.

A lot of programmers determine recursive functions as an easy way to achieve complete performance from the program.

Here is an example:

```
def result(example):
    if example == 0: return 0
    elif example == 1: return 1
    else: return result(example-1)+result(example-2)
```

Explanation of the program:

In the above program, we use a recursive function to find the Fibonacci numbers according to your input.

Here is a list of steps that we followed:

1) First of all, we created a function using the def reserved keyword and the function name along with a parameter.

2) This function uses a single parameter 'example' that is used to represent the number of Fibonacci numbers that need to be generated in the sequence.

3) In the next step, we created a control flow conditional statement that checks whether a number satisfies the Fibonacci sequence or not.

4) In the conditional statement, the result is always returned using the function.

5) In the next step, we use recursive mechanism to repeat the function logic and print the results.

6) The last step in the function informs to end the recursive function after it satisfies the parameter.

This is how the python uses functional programming to generate results. Python also supports higher-order functions such as Lambda for advanced operations.

How functional programming is essential for Machine Learning?

It is mandatory to learn functional modules in Python because a lot of third-party machine learning supportive libraries such as Pandas use functions to generate algorithms and graphs.

If you are not aware of defining custom functions it will become troublesome to generate unsupervised and supervised algorithms for a dataset.

Also, it is easy to articulate your logical thoughts into programming using functions. To improve your knowledge of function modules we suggest you read the documentation of various third-party libraries.

Higher-order functions

Python supports higher-order functions. Version 3 provides a lot of higher-order functions such as Lambda, filter, reduce.

This section will describe a lot of these in detail.

Follow along!

What is a higher-order function?

This works in the same way as a recursion. In higher-order functions, parameters are also functions.

You can use n number of functions as parameters and can obtain a function as a result.

Higher-order functions use the iterable concept to analyze different types of functions.

Python provides map() and reduce() functions by default. However, all other higher-order functions should be manually imported to make them work.

A lot of data science applications use higher-order functions to get perfect results.

a) Map

A map is a Python high order function that can be used to transform the position of the data set. In machine learning, the transformation of data points is a common phenomenon and is essential for developing regression algorithms.

Here is the format:

map (Enter the coordinates of data set here, Iteration points)

b) Filter

A filter is a Python higher-order function that can be used to predict the data points according to the scenarios given. This higher-order function is largely used in prediction algorithms.

A lot of video streaming websites such as YouTube and Netflix use filter to store user information to recommend the likewise videos.

Here is the format:

filter (Prediction analysis, Iteration)

3) Compose

Compose is a python higher-order function that can in a significant order input functions as parameters.

It can even use loops as a control flow statement to maintain the logical flow of the program. Compose is often used in advanced data analytics applications.

Here is the format:

compose(Enter the higher-order function here)

{

// Enter the logical statements here

}

Note:

Higher-order functions can use the same operating module operations as the remaining programming components.

4) Decorators

Higher-order functions are usually arranged syntactically as function parameters. However, decorators are used to syntactically used to arrange higher-order functions such as lambda functions in correct sequential order.

Decorators can take higher-order functions as arguments and output the instances.

Here is the format:

Decorator(Enter higher-order function 1, Enter higher-order function 2)

Decorators can also be used to implement coroutines and develop complex applications that can take coroutines as function arguments.

Decorators can also be very handy while dealing with any debugging and run-time errors.

To develop machine learning applications, it is always recommended to learn in-depth about different higher-order functions and the parameters they can regulate expressions with.

You can look at Python documentation to know about the different types of higher-order functions that are available.

With this, we have completed a brief introduction to functional programming in Python.

In the next chapter, we will discuss the operator module in detail.

Let us go!

Chapter 5: Operator module in Python

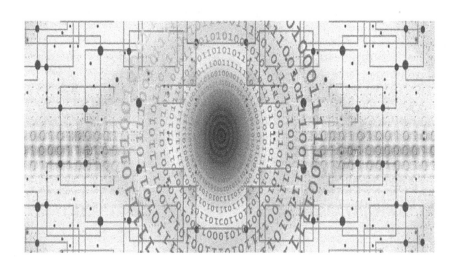

Operators are a mathematical entity which are usually used to combine expressions and statements. In regular mathematical expressions, operators can change the result that is going to obtain.

Python also provides an operator module that can explicitly impact the results that will be obtained. In this chapter, we will in detail discuss various operators that are available in the latest versions of Python.

Follow along!

Mathematical operators

Whenever we are learning a programming language it is essential to master mathematical operators because a lot of programs use mathematical calculations to perform the operations.

For example, to rotate an image in a photo viewer software programmers use transpose of mathematical matrices.

As we all know that mathematics has standard operations known as addition, subtraction, multiplication, and division. Python also provides a modulus operator to obtain the remainder of the mathematical operation.

In the next section, we will explain these mathematical operations with various examples.

Let us go!

Python code for Addition operator '+'

first = 2

second = 3

result = first+second

Result will output 5

Python code for Substraction operator '-'

first = 3

second = 2

result = first-second

Result will output 1

Python code for Multiplication operator '*'

first = 2

second = 3

result = first*second

```
# Result will output 6
# Python code for Division operator '/'
first = 6
second = 2
result = first/second
# Result will output 3
# Python code for Modulus operator '%'
first = 7
second = 6
result = first%second
# Result will output 1
```

Apart from these basic mathematical operations Python also provides an exponential operator ' * * '. We will give an example for your better understanding.

```
# Python code for Exponential operator '* *'
first = 5
second = 3
result = first * * second
# Result will output 125
```

Note: Python follows hierarchal rules to perform mathematical operations. Python also provides operator precedence to maintain a structural organization for the operations.

This is the sole reason why you need to use parenthesis to categorically group the operators.

Operator precedence

Operator precedence is an essential concept in programming languages while dealing with complex logical expressions. Python gives the exponential operator the highest precedence following by the multiplication, division and modulus operators.

Addition and Subtraction belong to the bottom layer of the operator precedence.

In the next section, we will in-depth explain about the comparison operators that are often used for determining a logic in an expression.

While dealing with complex machine learning data the machine needs to categorize and determine the data using these simple comparison operators. Follow along to know more about it.

Comparison Operators

Comparison operators are used in combining statements and to create logical expressions. There are a lot of comparison operators that can help you easily create logics for many mathematical functions.

In the next section, we will in detail discuss various comparison operators. We have four comparison operators. An example program is given to help you understand how comparison operators work.

Follow along!

a) Greater than

Here is an example to help you understand greater than operator:

```python
# Python code for Greater than Operator '>'
first = 5
second = 3
if ( first > second)
print(" This is the greater perspective")
else
print( " This is the lower perspective")
# Result will output the first statement
```

b) Less than

Here is an example to help you understand less than operator:

```python
# Python code for Greater than Operator '<'
first = 5
second = 3
if ( first < second)
print(" This is the lower perspective")
else
print( " This is the greater perspective")
# Result will output the second statement
```

c) Equal to

Here is an example to help you understand Equal to operator:

```python
# Python code for Greater than Operator '=='
```

```
first = 5
second = 3
if ( first == second)
print(" These two are the same")
else
print( " These two are not the same")
# Result will output the second statement
```

d) Not Equal to

Here is an example to help you understand Not Equal to operator:

```
# Python code for Greater than Operator '!='
first = 5
second = 3
if ( first != second)
print(" These two are not the same")
else
print( " These two are same")
# Result will output the first statement
```

With this, we have completed a small introduction to comparison operators. In the next section, we will in detail discuss Logical operators that are important for performing advanced data science operations.

Follow along!

Logical Operators

Logic is an important assignment component while dealing with complex programs. A lot of python programs consist of conditional and loop statements with logical operators.

There are fundamentally three logical operators which we will now discuss in detail in the next section.

a) and

This is a logical operator that can be used when you are looking forward to printing an expression when two statements are satisfied.

It is represented by 'and'.

Here is an example:

```
first = 2
second = 3
third = 5
if ( first ==2 and second==5)
print(" This is right")
else
print(" This is wrong")
```

Now, the program will check whether both first and second have the same values.

As the second variable is not satisfied ' This is wrong' will be displayed as the result.

b) or

This is a logical operator that can be used when you are looking forward to printing an expression when any one of the two statements are satisfied.

It is represented by 'or'.

Here is an example:

```
first = 2
second = 3
third = 5
if ( first ==2 or second==5)
print(" This is right")
else
print(" This is wrong")
```

Now, the program will check whether any one of the first and second have the same values.

As the first variable satisfies the condition ' This is right' will be displayed as the result.

c) not

This acts as a negation operator. That is, it will print when a condition is not satisfied. It is usually represented by 'not.

With this, we have completed a thorough explanation of operators in Python.

In the next chapter, we will start discussing advanced concepts related to iterations and comprehensions.

Let us go!

Chapter 6: Interaction and Generations in Python

In the previous chapters, we have discussed Python programming concepts that help you create basic programs. Functions and operators are fundamentals of python programming.

However, to create basic machine learning projects you need to dwell much deeper into Python. This section of this book involving three chapters will help you learn about interactions, iterations, and generators in detail.

A lot of these concepts are very essential to create effective machine learning models.

Follow along to know more about it.

What are Interactions?

Usually, Python consists of variables that store values in a memory location to use them whenever needed. Interactions are a special entity that helps you to create code that can change one set of variables when the other changes. You can implement interactions in Python using the SciPy library that is available.

Interactions are inspired by form statistics.

What are Comprehensions?

Comprehensions are a Python programming concept that can help you to create listing sequences such as dictionaries and lists effectively. Using comprehensions, you can automatically create a varied range of list values.

Comprehensions are a dynamic way to deal with complex. They use key and value to represent the instances that are produced.

How Interactions can be used in Python?

Python uses interactions and comprehensions to deal with complex listing programs. A lot of open-source software use interactions to develop brute-forcing tools for a faster dictionary attack. However, for the scope of this book, we will discuss the usage of interactions in Machine learning projects in depth in the next section.

Interactions in Machine learning

Interactions can be used instead of approximations to create machine learning algorithms.

You can use interactions to train the machine learning model. You can even try to change different variables to find out the correct interaction point.

Here is a program:

from sklearn

// This is where we need to import the functions from

regression = folds()

cross-validation()

interactions = (Enter the parameters here)

list()

// Create a list

if ()

[

  // create logic here

]

Explanation:

In this program, an interaction is created to give valid data points to the list.

In a machine learning environment, it is important to create an iterating comprehensive list to list out all the logical data points that are present.

You can also look out for different complex list operations to correlate with interactions and create effective machine learning programs.

What are Generations?

Generations are used to deal with higher-order functions automatically. They can argument the functions and can help you to iterate map and hash functions with simple values. Generator expressions are usually used in advanced Python expressions. They can be used with the help of a yield keyword in Python.

What to do next?

After further learning about interactions and comprehensions, we suggest you solve some advanced project scenarios to understand the essence of these concepts concerning machine learning. You can also use interactions to develop cross-validation techniques in Python. A lot of comprehensive machine learning algorithms use interactions to develop scenarios.

With this, we have completed a brief introduction to Interactions and comprehensions in Python. To further improve your skills we suggest you learn iterators and generators in Python and use all of them collaboratively to develop applications.

In the next chapter, we will in detail discuss iterations in Python programming.

Follow along!

Chapter 7: Iteration in Python

In this chapter, we will in detail explain to you iterative statements in Python. A lot of beginners get confused with the distinction between iterations and looping.

Always remember that looping is a branch of iterative statements. We will in detail discuss looping structures in the last chapter of this book. In this chapter, we will take a peek into the iterative statements that python possesses.

Follow along!

What are iterations?

Iterations in layman terms are simply programming objects that support repetition. Iterations can be used in implementing loops in different programming components and structures such as Tuples and dictionaries.

They are usually mistaken with for loop.

However, they represent 'for - in 'loop.

How to create iterations?

Python is a programming language that supports iterations effectively. It uses various higher-order functions to maintain the flow of iterations.

Also, remember that a lot of iterative principles can be achieved only if they follow certain principles.

a) Initialize an iterator

Usually, iterators are initialized with the help of an object. The _iter_ method is used as an initialization mechanism for iterators in Python.

A lot of machine learning models automatically call this method to initialize an iteration factor.

b) Using next in iterators

As explained initially, iterators are complex operations and often require processes that can forward the data.

Next is a function that can pre-process the information with the help of different iterative principles.

We can use for in loop to effectively coordinate the information present in iterators.

If you are not satisfied with the performance of the program, you can use a stopiteration() method to end the operation.

Here is a program:

class name

def iterative

-init-

Enter the parameters

object.c

stopiterative()

You can also use indexes and generators to further improve your iterative performance.

In the next section, we will in detail discuss the usage of iterators for machine learning projects.

Let us go!

How to use iterators for machine learning projects?

With the principle we have learned in the above section you can iteratively update the parameters for machine learning functions. As we already know that iteration is a set of repeated tasks you need to use it to implement real-world practical projects.

First of all, you need to understand the model you are working upon.

Any model that involves decision trees can be used for creating iterative parameters.

However, In Python Gradient descent is used extensively to create iterative algorithms.

You can also use cost functions to implement different models.

Here is an intuition for iterative programs:

1) Use loss functions create definitive iterative functions

2) You can also use parameters to minimize the overfitting problem of machine learning models.

3) You can also use several initialization parameters to increase the effectiveness of the machine learning model

4) Iterations can be further made effective using the local minimum and global minimum values.

All of these functionalities can be implemented using Max and min functions using the Pandas library in python.

In the below section, we give a python program to help you better understand the topic.

Here is the code:

import np

pandas iterator

max (Enter the parameters here)

min (Enter the parameters here)

// Use global variance to decrease the machine learning model effectiveness

You can also Use hyperparameters to better understand the iterative capabilities python provides. A lot of cross-validation techniques use iterators during the pre-processing procedure of machine learning.

With this, we have completed a brief introduction to iterators.

In the next chapter, we will in detail discuss generators with a lot of examples.

Follow along!

Chapter 8: Generators in Python

In the previous chapter, we have in detail discussed iteration principles with a couple of examples. In this chapter, we will further move forward and start discussing in detail about generators in Python.

This is a complex topic that is necessary to develop machine learning applications.

We suggest you to learn developing python generators using practical projects.

Follow along!

What are generators?

Generators are a lot similar to functions in Python. The only difference between functions and generators is the latter uses yield keyword to return the values.

So, for a simple trick just remember whenever you see a yield keyword in the Python programming example it is automatically a generator function.

Here is the format:

def {Enter the function name here}

yield

What are the generator objects?

Generator objects are formed when a generator function is created from scratch. They are usually implemented by the method structures that are present in the Python programming syntax.

Always remember that objects are object-oriented systematic structures and can result in mishaps if not coordinated well.

Here is the format:

generator {Enter the statement here}

object = // enter the generator expressions

What are the applications of generators?

Generators are usually used to deal with complex calculations. They can also be used to create iterable functions that are not coordinated well. They can be used to create complex Fibonacci sequences. Generators are extensively used to develop artificial intelligence applications.

A lot of embedded systems also use generators for faster implementation of hardware resources.

In the next section, we will in detail explain generator principles using a Fibonacci sequence example. Follow along!

Here is the code:

```
def fibonacciexam(parameters)

first,second = 3,4

// use generators

yield

x.first()

x.sexond()

// generator expression

yield.fib()

for (to display results)
```

In this example, the following implementation occurs:

1) First of all, you need to create a definition to initiate the procedure of creating a Fibonacci sequence. You can enter your desired values as input to start the procedure.

2) In the next step, you need to start using generators with the help of yield keyword to assign values to these variables.

Here, variables represent the iteration principle that we are going to look at in the next step.

3) Afterward, you need to create objects to represent the generator expression mechanism. You can use these objects to iterate through the variables and create a varied sequence that follows the Fibonacci sequence.

4) In the end, we again use generators to print the results.

With this program, we understood that generators can decrease the resources that need to be taken care of usually.

How generators can be used in machine learning?

Generators are an excellent component principle to train a scientific model. A lot of machine learning projects use a supervised model to perform operations. A supervised learning system hugely depends on preprocessing techniques to display varied results.

To decrease the overfitting problems in machine learning models generators can be used. You can use arrays to implement generators in Python.

In the next section, we will give an example that will help you to understand the advantages of generators in Python.

Here is the python code:

```
// create a list
List-name = ( Enter the values here)
Def machine
obj1 = gen(parameters)
Obj2 = gen.machine
yield
next(obj1)
```

You can use generators to create ranges between the data points. Here yield represents the generator expression. Machine learning is an extensive subject and learning generators will help you create models without any underfitting and overfitting errors.

With this, we have completed a small explanation about the generator.

In the next chapter, we will in detail discuss designing a project.

Follow along!

Chapter 9: How to code in Python?

This chapter is a simple introduction to basic python syntactical structures that can help you to code in Python. Python is a dynamically typed language and requires very fewer code blocks to define the logic.

Python is composed of different programmatically structures and is important to learn about them to write perfect code.

a) comments

Comments are an easy way to give information to the programmer while reading the code. They are usually followed after a # in the program. Comments are not compiled during run-time.

Here is an example:

this is a definition

def add(enter parameters here)

Comments are first developed to organize code structurally. However, with time comments have become an essential part of the programming.

b) literals

Literals are also known as constants in programming. These are values that can be assigned to a variable using an assignment operator. All literals can be replaced if wanted. Strings also fall under literals and can often be manipulated using different system functions.

Here is an example

a = 355

Here 355 is the literal that is being assigned to the variable 'a'

c) Variables

Variables are used as memory storage to store an assignment literal and use them whenever needed. Variables are important when dealing with functions and logical statements. You can easily change an assigned variable using logical statements.

Here is an example

first = 3

Here first is the name of the variable and 3 is the literal value that has been assigned to the variable. Always remember that variable can be assigned only through an assignment statement.

d) Datatypes

Datatypes are used to categorize variables that are created. It is important to assign a specified memory location whenever a variable is created. However, it is not feasible to create a constant size of memory location every time. So while creating a variable it is important to specify a data type. There are a lot of default data types such as integer, float, double and character.

Here is an example

int a=4788

// Here int is the data type

e) Conditional statements

Programming is composed of logical statements. When dealing with complex code we need to use control flow statements to get desired results. Python offers a lot of control flow statements such as conditionals and loops.

Conditional is a control flow statement where we have an option to choose by a logical evaluation. If—else is an easy way to represent a conditional statement.

Here is an example:

if(a>3)

{ #print the statement}

else

{ #pront another statement}

f) Operators

Operators are used to combine the statements to form expressions. In the previous chapter, we have in detail discussed the operator module. Always make sure you are aware of operator precedence before debugging the code.

g) Strings

Strings are one of the most important data types in python. Usually, we deal with a lot of string literals in common. Datasets are often combined in strong notions and can be manipulated using some of the string functions that are provided to python by default.

here is an example:

a = " This is a strong"

a.tolowercase()

Using this system function, you can convert string literals into lower case. You can check the documentation to find out different available string functions.

h) Exceptions

Python also provides advanced exception handling mechanism to deal with errors. Programs usually encounter errors while they are running. It is important to show the errors to the end-user to help them understand the mistake they are doing.

To make this happen we use try, catch blocks to enter the exceptions and their error output.

i) Lists

Python handles multiple data using the available structures. There are different data structures such as lists, tulles, and dictionaries to handle multi-dimensional data. It is important to master these if you are trying to develop machine learning applications.

With this, we have explained some of the basic programmatically concepts that are necessary to start coding in Python. In the next section, we will in detail discuss coding using an IDE.

How to start coding in Python?

In the previous chapter, we have explained about using a text editor to create python programs. However, python programs can be written using an Integrated development environment. In this section, we use PyCharm to explain about starting to code with Python.

Step 1:

Open the software and click on the "create new" button to open a new python file. You can even create new classes and interfaces for easy maintenance of the python project.

Step 2:

After creating a new python file, you can start writing code. In the IDE you can easily insert conditionals and loops using different pre-installed functions. You can also create templates and packages on a one click

Step3:

After creating a program, it is now time to start compiling in the IDE. You can just click on the Run button to start the Python interpreter to look at your code. If any errors are present, they will be displayed.

Step 4:

You can interlink these individual codes to start creating packages. You can use inheritance to use methods that have been used by python classes

Step 5:

Click the save button to save all the code information that has been created.

What should you remember?

Always, make sure that you are following the Python programming conditions. Python doesn't support case sensitive statements and there is no use of indentation spaces. Python is also easy to maintain and organize. However, we recommend you maintain a good coding structure to help you look back at your code without any confusion.

With this, we have completed a brief introduction to starting code with Python. There are a lot of resources to further enhance your skills. You can look at our book in this previous module to increase your Python programming knowledge.

In the next chapter, we will start discussing a sample project.

Let us go!

Chapter 10: Planning and design a project in Python

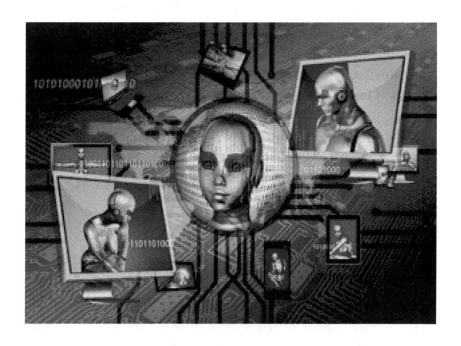

In the previous chapter, we have learned about basic programming structures. This chapter will help you know how to start creating a project with an example.

This chapter and the next chapter are practical experimentation with a sample project to increase your Python skills.

Follow along!

Know the purpose of your project

Before developing the project, first introduce the purpose of the project, so that everyone will focus on it when studying.

The development objectives of this project are as follows:

(1) Write a project to remotely control the computer to do a remote shutdown or restart.

(2) Review the basic knowledge of Python that you have learned before.

(3) Master the general process of project development. When receiving a software project, one should not blindly do it immediately but should do it step by step according to the process of project development.

Project making procedure

Developing a project from scratch is a complex procedure and is often achieved only when certain procedures are followed. A lot of experienced programmers use the following blueprint we are going to use now to develop Python projects. The process is mainly as follows.

(1) Demand analysis.

(2) Design.

(3) Writing.

(4) Testing.

(5) Use.

(6) Maintenance.

If you don't know these steps, get a project and do it according to your feelings. Large projects will inevitably be done in a chaotic way, which will eventually affect the efficiency of project development and the ultimate benefits.

When developing a project, the development steps are very important. Everyone should start from small projects and form good and standard habits.

⌷OBJ⌷ Concept of Demand Analysis

Requirement analysis is a detailed analysis of the functions to be required by a project. For example, the purpose, scope, definition, and function of a project are analyzed, in other words, the requirements of the project are positioned.

Application Examples of Requirement Analysis for this Project

This project is to make a Python small software that can remotely control restart or shutdown functions of a computer. The programming idea is as follows. First, you need to know how to control the restart and shutdown of the computer locally through Python, and then you need to know how to send messages to Python programs remotely.

Here, Python's standard library can be used to control the restart or shutdown of the local computer. To achieve remote control, e-mail can be used as a remote-control channel. For example, Python can automatically log into the mailbox to detect mail.

When sending a shutdown command to this mailbox, if Python detects a shutdown command, Python directly sends a command to control the shutdown of the machine.

The so-called "requirement analysis" here refers to functional requirement analysis, that is, clarifying which functions the project needs to realize.

Secondly, this is not a complete requirement analysis document, but a draft requirement analysis during actual development.

This step is very necessary and it is recommended to master it.

For a complete requirement analysis document, you can search the corresponding template on the search engine for reference and compilation.

If it is not commercial software development, writing a complete requirement analysis document is not a necessary step.

The following is a brief demand analysis of the project:

(1) Control the shutdown of the local computer through Python code.

(2) Log into the mailbox through Python (of course, other remote-control channels can also be selected).

(3) Monitor and read the mail content of the designated mailbox through Python.

(4) Realize the function of mail sending through Python.

(5) The core business logic processing part (such as how to monitor, if judge when to shut down or restart, etc.).

After understanding the above functional requirements, the corresponding code can be written step by step.

[OBJ] Implementation of Simple Code

As mentioned above, to restart or shut down the computer remotely, Python must first control the computer to restart or shut down locally.

The following is the realization of this function. For the first time, only Python can control the computer to restart or shut down locally.

This development is also called the first development and can be used as the first version of the simple program in the development process of small software.

If you want to control the local computer to restart or shut down, you can use the os.system () method and pass in relevant Shell instructions.

You can control the computer to shut down through a Shell command shutdown, and you can also control the computer to restart through a Shell command ' -r'.

Here is the Python code:

import os

⬚# shutdown the system

os.system{ Enter the parameters here}

After executing the above code, the computer will automatically shut down.

If you want to use Python code to control the restart of your local computer, you can do this by following Python code:

import os

restart the system

os.r(Enter the parameters here)

After executing the above code, the computer will restart automatically.

Therefore, the simple version of the code is as follows:

{Use import functions here}

("Please enter what you want to do: shutdown input 1, restart input 2")

Note 1 enclosed in double quotation marks.

Because the input is a string instead of the number

if (result = = "1"):

shut down { Get the parameters here}

 print ("shutdown instruction is ready")

```
elif (result = = "2"):
# Restart os.system { Get the parameters here}
print ("restart instruction is ready")
else:
print ("no operation performed")
```

After executing the above program, we will be prompted to enter the desired operation, as follows:

Please enter the operation you wish to perform:

shutdown

input 1,

restart

input 2

If we want to shut down, we can enter 1 and press enter.

 If you want to restart, you can enter 2 and press Enter.

 If you enter additional information and press enter, nothing will be done.

For example, entering 3 and pressing enter key will output the following information:

Please enter what you want to do:

shut down

input 1,

restart input 2

If you enter 2 and press Enter, the restart command will be executed as follows:

Please enter the operation you wish to perform:

shutdown input 1 and restart input 22.

The restart command was executed successfully.

Subsequently, the computer will be shut down and restarted automatically within one minute.

Similarly, if after executing the above code, enter 1 and press enter key, the shutdown operation will be executed.

Here, how to control the restart and shutdown of the local computer through Python code is realized.

This is the first version of the small target software, i.e. the simple version.

The final target has not been reached, so further development is needed.

📷 Debugging during Development

Sometimes, when writing software, there will be certain errors and problems. The process of trying to solve these problems is called debugging.

When we develop this project, we will also encounter various problems. It doesn't matter.

We just need to find out where the problem is and improve the corresponding procedures. Debugging is often carried out during project development, and it is difficult to develop the program perfectly at one time.

For example, when you write a program in the mail reading phase if the waiting time for the operation is too long, you will often encounter some errors that cannot be connected. At this time, you can solve the problem by re-executing the login code.

This process is a debugging process.

Similarly, when you encounter other problems, you should try your best to locate the problem first, and then compare with the above procedures, carefully observe which place or details the problem is.

If you still can't think out, you can put the error prompt into the search engine to find out and see if it can be solved.

In short, when you encounter problems, think independently and try to solve these problems independently can make your programming ability stronger.

[OBJ] Concept of Program Packaging

The process of turning the written program code into software that can be directly executed is called program packaging.

For example, scripts written now can only be run in the Python editor.

After they are packaged into software, they can be run directly in the operating system without the support of the Python editor.

Method of Packaging Python Programs

Readers can use some tools to package Python programs into executable application software.

In Python, tools commonly used for packaging include py2exe, Pyinstaller, etc. These tools do not need to be mastered completely, so everyone can choose a tool that they think is suitable.

This book will introduce how to package Python programs through Pyinstaller.To use Pyinstaller, you need to install it first.

Here, you can install Pyinstaller directly using pip. First, open the cmd command-line interface, and then enter the instructions. The Pyinstaller is installed through the "pip install pyinstaller" instruction and only needs to wait for the installation to be completed.

After the installation is completed, the installation success prompt message will appear.

In addition, readers can see the installed tool file pyinstaller.exe in the Scripts directory under the Python installation directory.

⑦Next, you can use the Pyinstaller tool to package Python programs into application software.

For example, the path of the complete program of this project is "D:/ sample/project.py" and the Python installation directory of my computer is "D:/Python". Therefore, the Python program of this project can be packaged through the following cmd instructions:

D: \ > d: \ python\ scripts \installer

d: \sample\ project.py

⑦The successfully packaged executable program can be found in the D:/dist directory. The sample folder is the software folder related to the project.py program that has just been packaged and generated.

⑦The file with the ".exe" extension is the executable file generated after packaging. Double-click the file to run directly.

At this time, the current computer can be remotely controlled to restart or shut down only by opening the program, so long as the "shutdown" or "restart" instruction is sent to the designated mailbox.

As can be seen, the currently packaged program needs to rely on many files. Because there are too many dependent files, it is very inconvenient to migrate packaged programs to other computers to run.

In fact, it is also possible to package all the dependent files into an. exe file, just add the -F parameter when packaging.

At the same time, a cmd interface will appear after the software is opened. In some cases, you don't want the software to have this cmd interface, but you can also directly shield it through the -w parameter when packaging, which will be much more beautiful in some cases.

Next, I will show you how to package all the dependent files into a .exe file without the cmd interface.

The packaged cmd instructions are as follows:

After packaging, a separate. exe file will be generated in the D:/dist directory. Readers can directly migrate the file to other computers.

Even if other computers do not have a good Python development environment, double-click the. exe file to execute it (but it is better to close the antivirus software to avoid interference from accidental killing).

In addition, since the -w parameter is added during packaging, the cmd interface will not be displayed when running the software, because the cmd interface has been shielded by the -w parameter.

If you want to display a cmd interface, do not add -w parameter when packing. Running the software can realize the function of remotely controlling the computer to shut down or restart through e-mail.

With this, we have completed a brief introduction to Python project creation.

In the next chapter, we will further discuss this practical project.

Follow along!

Chapter 11: Practical Project in python

In the previous chapter, we have discussed ways to design a project. In this project, we will in detail explanation about the implementation of a practical project with a lot of background information followed by Python code.

Follow along carefully.

Maintenance and Improvement

⬜It has been successfully implemented to control the shutdown or restart of the computer through Python, but it cannot meet all requirements. Therefore, it is necessary to solve this defect: the program can not only control the shutdown or restart of the local computer but also remotely control the shutdown or restart of the computer through the network.

After discovering the defects of the old version, the process of developing the new version is the maintenance and improvement of the software.

[OBJ] *Remote Control Channel*

[?]If you want to remotely control the shutdown or restart of the computer, the local computer needs networking. After networking, you also need to choose a remote-control channel, such as Gmail, web page or e-mail.

Controlling Python to Operate Computer 1 via Mail

As long as it can communicate with remote, it can be used as a channel for remote control. Therefore, there are many channels for remote control. In this project, the mail is chosen as the channel tool for remote control.

[OBJ] *Controlling Python to Operate Computer 2 via Mail*

This project uses e-mail as a remote-control channel to realize remote control of computers. It can be seen that the user sends corresponding instructions to the e-mail, then the instructions are transmitted to Python code (the specified instructions can be monitored regularly by Python), and finally, the local computer is controlled to execute corresponding operations by Python code.

Therefore, the following parts need to be developed in turn:

(1) Log into the mailbox through Python (of course, other remote-control channels can also be selected).

(2) Monitor and read the mail content of the designated mailbox through Python.

(3) Realize the function of mail sending through Python (not required).

(4) the core business logic processing part.

First of all, you need to prepare a mailbox. Because the port and use of Gmail are different from other mailboxes, here you can use Rediff mail for operation.

Here, the author has prepared a Rediff mailbox (account number or password may be modified later, and the modified code cannot be used, so everyone should register a mailbox of their own).

Account number: example@rediffmail.com

Password: sample123

Log in to your mailbox on the web page and make some settings.

The default SMTP and POP3 are closed, but SMTP is required to send mail through Python code, POP3 is required to read mail through Python code, so these two items need to be opened first.

You can select the "Settings-Client pop/imap/smtp" option in the mailbox personal center control panel.

As you can see, the default POP3 and SMTP are turned off, so you need to select the "on" radio button and save it.

⏎After opening, you can log in to the mailbox using Python code.

As can be seen, the default POP3 server and SMTP server information of Rediff mailbox are as follows.

POP3 server: pop.rediff.com.

SMTP Server: smtp.rediff.com.

Next, I'll show you how to log in to your mailbox using the Python code.

The purpose of logging into the mailbox is different, and the modules used are also different.

If the purpose of logging into the mailbox is to send mail, you can call SMTP () under smtplib to establish a mail object, and then call login () method under the mail object to log in.

If the purpose of logging into the mailbox is to check mail, you can call POP3 () under poplib to establish a mail object, and then call the user () method and pass_ () method under the object to set the account and password when logging into the mailbox. After setting, you can log in.

Next, you can enter the following code to demonstrate how to log in to the mailbox:

The key parts have been commented:

1. log in to the mailbox for sending mail

import { Enter the library}

establish a mail object through SMTP (), the parameters in which are the SMTP server address of the corresponding mailbox

smpt.call()

Through the above exercises, everyone should have mastered how to log into the mailbox using Python code. It should be noted that the modules and methods used to log in to the mailbox are different depending on the purpose of use.

Next, I'll show you how to monitor and read the mail content of the specified mailbox through Python.

If you want to read the mail information of the specified mailbox through Python code, you need to log in to the corresponding mailbox through POP3 first, then call stat () to obtain statistical information.

You can specify to return the first few lines of mail information through top () and decode the returned information.

After decoding, the decoded information can be converted into recognizable mail information by email.message_from_string (), and then the recognizable mail information can be processed by email.header.decode_header (), and the required mail information can be read out after processing.

For example, if you need to read the title of the latest email, it can be implemented by the following code, and the key parts have been given detailed comments:

print (statistics) (Here is the values)

emailmsg = mail. top (statistics [0], 0)

⬚print(emailmsg)

⬚for I in emailmsg [1]: newmsg. append (I.decode ())

> > > # view decoded information >

⬚title = decode _ header (myemailmsg ["subject"])

Through the above code, the mail information can be read directly. At this time, you can log into the mailbox of the webpage version to verify whether it is correct.

After logging into the mailbox of the webpage version, you can see the information on the latest email.

⬚It can be seen that the message title of the latest mail is "I am a test mail", which is consistent with the results read and output in the code. Therefore, the mail information in the mailbox has now been successfully read through the code.

Next, let's introduce how to realize the function of mail sending through Python. This part of the program is not necessary for this project.

The purpose of this project is to realize the remote control of the computer through the remote channel of e-mail, which only requires Python to monitor the instruction information in the e-mail.

The link to sending e-mail can be realized by Python code or traditional e-mail, so this part is not necessary. Of course, learning the function of this part and writing it in the program can make the project more perfect.

If you need to realize the function of mail sending through Python, you can log in to the e-mail box by SMTP first, then set the content of the e-mail to be sent through MIMEText under email.mime.text, then call sendmail () under the logged-in e-mail object to realize the mail sending, and finally call close () under the e-mail object to realize the connection closing.

For example, the following code can be used to send e-mail messages:

mail.login ('credentials',' password') (235, B' ok authenticated')

content = mimetext ('I am the specific content of the mail! This email is mainly used to test whether it can be sent. ")

content ['from'] =' sample@rediffmail.com'

content ['to'] =' example@rediffmail.com, abcdefg'

After running the above code, the mail is sent to the specified mailbox through Python code. At this time, the receiver's mailbox will display the relevant email information just sent.

⯑It can be seen that the relevant mail has been received in the receiver's mailbox. If you can't find it in your inbox, you can try to find it in the trash.

To avoid entering the trash, you can add the sender's email address to the white list.

Now, the related functions can be realized through Python code. Next, we will integrate the above functions to complete the development of the whole project.

At present, the core business logic processing part of this project is written. The main idea is: firstly, establish a function to control the shutdown of the local computer, a function to control the restart of the local computer, a function to read the header of the first email of the designated email, a function to send the corresponding content to the designated email, etc.

Then write a while loop in which you log in to the specified email regularly and read the header of the first email.

If the title is certain specified information, the corresponding custom function is called to perform the corresponding operation, for example, the title is "shutdown", and the shutdown function can be called to control the shutdown of the local computer.

After performing the corresponding operation, call the mail sending function to send a new mail to the specified mailbox. It should be avoided that the title of the new mail is the same as the specified information defined by us.

In this way, when the software monitors the title of the latest mail in the mailbox next time, it will not perform the previous operation endlessly, because the title of the latest mail has been reset at this time.

The complete code of this project is as follows:

Defrestart (): importos

restart os.system ('shutdown-r')

print ("restart command executed successfully")

mail = poplib.pop3 ('pop.rediff.com') mail.user ('weiweitest789 @ rediff.com')

detect time.sleep (5) every 5s

While the program is running, wait for remote instructions.

As long as the above program is executed on the local computer, the computer will always listen to remote instructions. For example, the computer in the home runs the above program now, but you are in the office.

At this time, you can send an email titled "Restart" to weiweitest789@rediff.com (that is, the email address monitored in the program), and the computer in the home will automatically restart. If you send an email titled "Shut Down" to the email, the computer in the home will automatically shut down. At this time, you can remotely control the computer to restart or shut down.

For example, now send a message titled "Shut Down" remotely to the email address (weiweitest789@rediff.com) monitored in the program. While the program is running, wait for the remote instruction shutdown instruction to execute successfully.

Then the computer automatically performs the shutdown operation.

After rebooting, log in to the receiving mailbox and find the mail message. The mail titled "shutdown" was just sent manually and remotely. when the local program detects the title "shutdown", it automatically calls the send () function to send a reset mail, i.e. the mail titled "test" and then controls the computer to perform the shutdown operation. So far, this project has been successfully written and its functions have been realized.

[OBJ] Project Implementation and Summary

So far, this project has been fully realized. In the process of writing this small project, everyone knew the basic process of project development and went through it completely. I hope everyone will have a project management awareness when receiving software projects.

Developing projects according to standard procedures will greatly improve the development efficiency of large projects. You these ideas to develop your projects in Python. All the best!

In the next chapter, we will in detail discuss Machine learning.

Let us go!

Chapter 12: Machine learning in Python

Machine learning is a branch of computer science that extracts valuable information from the huge chunks of data that is available. It uses various computer science and statistics principles to create a well versed artificial intelligent application.

Machine learning has been a prominent field in research for decades.

However, in the 21st century with the development of high-level computing machines, Machine learning applications rose into an all-time high. Almost all web applications use Machine learning algorithms to suggest recommendations for the user.

This chapter is a detailed step-by-step material that will help you understand the importance of Machine learning in day-to-day life and will also introduce you to using Python as a supportive language to develop Machine learning applications.

Follow along!

Machine learning in Day-to-Day life

Before starting with the technical stuff, we will give a real-world example to help you understand the importance of machine learning algorithms in real life.

Imagine using a virtual assistant such as Siri/Google Assistant to ask your questions regarding the best restaurant in your surroundings. When you ask this question, the virtual assistant analyzes huge data that is present and selects a restaurant according to your requirements. This is how an actual search query works. Machine learning adds a layer of functionality to it. It monitors how you have reacted to the result and improves itself and produces better results the next time.

So, to say in a single sentence:

" Machine learning is a computer learning scenario where the machine improves itself with time"

Applications of Machine Learning

At the initial stages, Machine learning is used to automate decision making with the help of various algorithms that have been developed by then. This exact branch of machine learning is known as supervised learning.

There is also another branch of machine learning known as unsupervised learning where the machine generates new algorithms by itself according to the datasets provided.

For example, Machine learning algorithms are used to develop Spam filter mails in the 2000s. Mail developers used all the spam words that they have collected and made an algorithm to automatically send the suspected mail to the spam folder.

You may wonder that this is just a normal spam filter application but this spam filter software automatically updates itself with the new spam filter database.

Machine learning systems learn all the way while doing the work they are told to do.

In the next section, we will in detail discuss the applications of Machine learning in detail.

Follow along!

a) They are used in Medical clinical analysis

Machine learning can be used to develop applications that can detect the medical tumor or the skin diseases that patients are suffering by checking the thousands of clinical photos that are collected. They can also be used to conduct a differential diagnosis for the patient at the same time.

b) Security

Machine learning can be used to develop applications that can increase the security of online transactions. A lot of fraudulent credit card operations follow a pattern and it is often easy by machine learning algorithms to block the fraudulent transactions.

c) Image processing

Machine learning can be used to develop applications that can detect your face. This branch of machine learning is known as Deep learning and is quite famous among the industry.

d) Recommendations

A lot of websites rely on cloud user data to give the same recommendations that the users may like. E-commerce websites Like amazon analyze the user data and provide recommendations that the users may likely buy. All these recommendations are generated using different machine learning algorithms that the websites use.

5) Categorizing

Machine learning algorithms can also be used to categorize the data that is collected using different topics. This is known as the regression algorithm and can be very useful if done in the right way for e-commerce and streaming applications.

With this, we have completed a brief introduction that explains the application of Machine learning. In the next section, we will discuss the usage of Python in Machine learning applications.

Let us go!

Why Python is considered best for Machine Learning?

Python is considered best because it consists of libraries for every available computer stream. There are libraries for statistics and visualization that can be explicitly used for data analysis. Python also is very interactive and can interact with the data points using software such as Jupyter notebook. Also, remember that machine learning is a computational process that highly depends on the iteration levels. Python is an interactive language and is thus considered the best programming language for machine learning.

Here are some of the Python libraries that are essential for developing Machine learning Projects.

a) Scikit Learn

This is a fundamental machine learning library consisting of different famous machine learning algorithms. Scikit learn consists of a documentation file where there is sufficient information about every algorithm that is present.

It is particularly famous among computer scientists because it curates a lot of essential algorithms in one library.

A lot of machine learning algorithms present in scipy can be easily deployed to your software.

First of all, install the scikit learn in your system using the following command:

root @ tony : pipi install { Enter the dependencies} scikit

What are the dependencies that are required?

You need to install Anaconda a Python module for making sci-kit learn work.

Anaconda consists of a lot of Python modules that are essential to run machine learning algorithms.

b) Jupyter notebook

This is a python tool that will help you to run the program code in the browser.

It is important to note that Jupyter also supports different languages. So, if you have any code of other languages you can integrate it with python to get desirable results.

C) NumPy

As said before, Machine learning is a branch of computer science that is a combination of mathematics, statistics and computer science.

To make efficient machine learning programs it is essential to use statistical algorithms that NumPy offers. NumPy is a python library that consists of multidimensional arrays and higher-order mathematical functions. NumPy is usually used to represent or find out data points in the data set.

d) SciPy

Machine learning in the initial stages is a complete scientific field. A lot of algorithms are developed to find out an easy way to deal with programming high computing machines. SciPy is a python library that deals with scientific computing. It is important because it consists of higher-order mathematical functions that can be used in deep learning applications. SciPy modules can also be used to create sparse matrices.

e) matplotlib

It is important to visualize the data while developing machine learning applications. A lot of statistical graphs can be used to create visualization such as histograms and scatters. Data set can be visualized using the matplotlib in Python. This library can help you to provide an interactive environment while dealing with huge chunks of data.

f) pandas

Data analysis is also a branch of machine learning and requires pandas to analyze the data by using data frames. Using pandas, you can create programs that can query and select the data.

It is important to master pandas to analyze CSV files.

These are some of the important Python libraries that are essential to master machine learning.

It is also important to remember that Python 3 is mandatory to run all of these libraries mentioned. So, make sure you are aware of all the Python 3 programming basics.

In the next section, we will explain a simple example that will help you understand the process of machine learning.

It is quite theoretical for now. However, you can always fill your gaps with research.

Python is still iterating and is not forward compatible, which also causes the current Python to split into two major versions, namely Python 2.X and Python 3.x.

Although it is not yet grammatically two languages, the two codes cannot be mixed, and the choice of the version is also the first thing to be determined when learning to use Python.

Previously, it was generally believed that Python 2.X had a longer development time and more and more mature support libraries in various aspects. many people recommended starting with this version.

However, as the Python team announced that it would stop maintaining Python 2.X in 2020, all major communities have already started the migration from 2.X to 3.X, so it is more recommended to choose 3.X when learning Python now.

Python is a general programming language, and its syntax satisfies Turing completeness, which cannot be fully explained here. However, if you are familiar with the C or Java language, you can think of Python's syntax as a highly condensed version of them. In addition to the above-mentioned need not make type declarations, Python also lacks curly braces to indicate scope and semicolons at the end of statements.

At the same time, the indentation in Python is not only a code specification but also a mandatory requirement at the syntax level.

If you have a language foundation and remember these differences, you should be able to use Python skillfully and quickly.

Strategy for learning Machine learning with Python

Generally speaking, there are two ways to practice algorithm theory. One is to implement the algorithm with code by oneself. The other is to make full use of the convenience of the tool, quickly understand and grasp the existing resources, and then begin to solve practical problems.

I think it is very difficult to decide on whether to build wheels again. Each method has its advantages and disadvantages.

After the rapid development of machine learning in recent years, it has accumulated very rich open resources.

By making full use of these resources, you can quickly master and solve practical problems even if you did not know this field before.

First is the programming language, we choose Python. In the past few years, Python and R languages have maintained a dual situation in the field of machine learning.

It can be generally considered that the industry prefers Python while academia prefers R.

However, with the development of technology, Python language has become the undisputed "eldest brother" in the field of machine learning, especially after the support library required for in-depth learning in recent years has been implemented in Python without exception.

Due to the popularity of machine learning, Python even has the strength to compete with the traditional programming languages C and Java and tends to lag in the ranking of many programming languages.

The next step is to support the library Numpy. Machine learning involves a large number of mathematical operations such as matrix operations.

Fortunately, Python has two major characteristics, one is flexibility, and the other is a large number of libraries. Numpy is a professional support library specially designed for scientific computing in Python and is well-known in the industry.

Not only machine learning, but also other scientific fields such as mathematical operations involved in astrophysics, either directly use NumPy or build higher-level functional libraries based on NumPy.

Finally, is the algorithm library Scikit-Learn. There are many Python-based machine learning algorithm libraries. However, Scikit-Learn is always at the top of the list.

It not only has a complete range of types but also can find the corresponding API for the machine learning algorithms available on the market. It is simply a "supermarket of machine learning algorithms". Besides, it is well packaged and has a clear structure.

You can complete the call of a complex algorithm through a few simple lines of code. It is a good introduction to the field of machine learning, and it is also an advanced magic weapon.

Famous Machine Learning Algorithms

Common machine learning algorithms are as follows:

(1) Linear Regression Algorithm

This is the most basic machine learning algorithm, but although sparrows are small and have all five organs, this algorithm can be called the "Hello World" program in the field of machine learning algorithms. It uses linear methods to solve regression problems.

(2) Logistic regression classification algorithm

This is the "twin brother" of the linear regression algorithm. Its core idea is still the linear method, but a "waistcoat" named Logistic function is set up, which enables it to solve classification problems.

(3) KNN classification algorithm

This algorithm is the only one of the classification algorithms introduced in this book that does not rely on mathematical or statistical models but purely relies on "life experience".

It solves the classification problem through the idea of "finding the nearest neighbor". Its core idea has a far-reaching relationship with the consensus mechanism in blockchain technology.

(4) Naive Bayesian classification algorithm

This is a set of algorithms that can refresh your world outlook. It believes that the results are not deterministic but probabilistic. What you see in front of your eyes is only the results with the greatest probability.

Of course, the algorithm is used to solve the problem. Naive Bayesian classification algorithm solves the classification problem.

(5) Support Vector Machine Classification Algorithm

If the Logistic regression classification algorithm is the most basic linear classification algorithm, then the support vector machine is the highest form of linear classification algorithm and is also the most "mathematical" machine learning algorithm. The algorithm uses a series of stunning mathematical techniques to map linearly indivisible data points into linearly separable data points and then uses the simplest linear method to solve the problem.

(6)K-means clustering algorithm

Supervised learning is a mainstream method of machine learning at present, but sample marking needs a lot of labor costs, which is prone to the problem of large sample accumulation scale but insufficient marking. Unsupervised learning is a machine learning algorithm that does not rely on labeled samples.

(7) Neural Network Classification Algorithm

Many people think that this algorithm is bionic, and the object of imitation is our brain. The neural network classification algorithm is also the starting point of the popular depth learning algorithm.

With this, we have completed a thorugh introduction to machine learning using Python.

In the next chapter, we will in detail discuss about classes and objects in Python.

Follow along!

Chapter 13: How to create a Class in python?

Object-oriented programming is an essential feature in the Python programming language. Even with the presence of the functional programming paradigm in Python a lot of developers like to use object-oriented mechanisms for developing programs.

There are a lot of reasons that make developers choose object-oriented programming over functional. Machine learning experts should be quite aware of object and class creation when dealing with algorithms.

This chapter is a comprehensive introduction to object-oriented programming basics.

Let us start!

How is it different from procedural programming?

Procedural programming is a paradigm where problems are solved using reusable code segments known as functions. It is often difficult to insert new logic or data to the already created code. In a machine learning environment, it is often important to automatically rearrange the code segments to give the best results.

This is the reason why machine learning enthusiasts should implement resources that will help you to extend into an object-oriented model whenever needed.

How does object orientation work?

Object-oriented programming uses a different philosophy that separates like-minded objects into categories. Using these categories, you can individually change functionalities that are required.

Apart from easier code maintenance, they can also be used to maintain the unity of the functions.

We will now in detail discuss classes and objects from a data scientist perspective.

What are Classes and Objects?

From a programmer's perspective, classes are a blueprint that are developed to deal with objects easily.

In a class, we will usually group like-minded variables, methods, and constructors to easily work with them.

When dealing with small projects procedural programming techniques are feasible.

However, as the size of the project expands, we need to write a lot of code that does the same thing from a different perspective.

To counter this problem Classes and Objects are developed, by which we can easily inherit the parent classes and use them in our projects.

What do classes consist of?

Classes consist of methods that can do a certain task. There are global and local variables in a class that can be used according to the situation.

All these methods and variables can be used as an object instance by the programmer.

How to define a class?

In Python, unlike Java, you need to store classes using a Python file. In java programming language programmers usually save separate class files with a .class extension. However, Python makes things simple by using the same .py format. In the next section, we will use an example that will help you understand the creation of a class in Python.

To master object-oriented programming, we first need to understand the basic theories and concepts of object-oriented programming.

This section will introduce the basic theories and concepts of object-oriented programming in detail.

Object-Oriented scenarios in real life

In the world we live in, any specific thing can be regarded as an object, and each object can handle some things or have some static characteristics.

For example, each specific person can be regarded as an object. This object can handle some things, such as eating, singing, writing, etc.

Some functions realized by this object can be called methods of this object. Similarly, this object has some static features, such as hair, arms, body, etc. You can call the static features of this object the attributes of this object.

Thus, the method is dynamic and the attribute is static.

If Tony is regarded as an object A and Christopher as object b, Tony and Christopher can communicate and pass on some information. In the object-oriented thinking method, messages can also be transmitted and communicated between objects, so that each object can form a powerful and complex network, thus realizing some complex architectures and functions.

According to the commonness of various objects in nature, objects can be abstracted into classes, and any object must belong to a certain class. Objects are concrete and classes are abstract.

For example, there are now the following objects:

Object A: Tony is a person.

Object B: Tony

Object C: A specific orange

Object d: A specific apple

According to the commonness between object a and object b, object a and object b can be abstracted as human, which is called human for short.

According to the commonness between object c and object d, object c and object d can be abstracted as fruit class.

Thus, objects A, B, C and D all have their own classes. Of course, the commonness among object A, object B, object C, and object D can also be extracted and abstracted into a class of biology.

In object-oriented programming, we can divide a complex software into various required classes according to requirements, and then write various methods and attributes.

When it is used specifically, it can be instantiated into specific objects directly according to the class, and then relevant functions can be implemented.

The process of instantiation is the process of transforming abstract things into concrete things. After instantiation, the software's relatively complex architecture and functions can be implemented using related objects.

It can be seen that programming through object-oriented thinking can make the development of programs closer to the real world and realize complex functions and architectures more convenient.

Advanced Concepts

Through the above introduction, I believe everyone has a simple understanding of the basic idea of object-oriented, and this section will specifically introduce how to apply the object-oriented method to program design.

For example, to realize a large project, you can divide the project into different components, treat each different component as each class, then program these components separately, and finally assemble each component into a large project.

This approach can control the project as a whole and make the development of the project more efficient.

Object-oriented programming is different from process-oriented programming. Process-oriented programming is to write programs according to the specific process of this project. This method is suitable for writing small and medium-sized programs, while for larger projects, it can be handled with object-oriented thinking.

If large projects are also developed according to the process-oriented programming idea, the efficiency will be lower and the object-oriented programming idea will be used for development.

It is only necessary to divide the project into various classes (i.e. abstract forms of various parts of large projects), then develop various classes, and then combine various classes.

When you need to use it, you can directly create specific objects according to classes, and then implement corresponding specific functions through each object.

Class is a relatively important concept in object-oriented, and object is also a relatively important concept in object-oriented.

The concepts of class and object are usually mentioned together, and this section will show you how to use Python to implement classes and objects.

How to create classes?

Classes are abstractions of commonness between certain objects.

In popular terms, a class is a synthesis of many identical things. For example, a good song, a piece of calligraphy and a good-looking novel are all the objects.

You can think about the commonness of these things and what can be used to summarize them?

They can be summarized by a class called "literature and art". Literature and art do not represent any specific thing, it is an abstract concept.

In a word: class is the abstraction of an object, and the object is the concrete expression of class, which is also called the instance of the class.

For example, as we have just introduced, the objects of a beautiful song, calligraphy, and a beautiful novel can abstract the category of literature and art.

When we say literature and art, it must be abstract, so the category is abstract of the object.

Use of Classes in Python

In Python, if you want to implement object-oriented programming, you first need to divide the corresponding classes and then write the specific code to implement the classes.

If you want to create a class in Python, you can do this in the following format:

Class Name ():

{

  Enter the implementation procedure here

}

For example, if you want to create a human class, you can do this by following the code:

class man:

⊠pass

Here, the pass statement has no practical significance but is called a placeholder statement to ensure the integrity of the program.

After running the above program, we can make the following input:

>>> print （man）

As you can see, the current corresponding output result is "class ......", indicating that man is a class at this time.

Application Examples of Objects

Generally speaking, classes cannot be directly used to implement related functions and operations, because classes are abstract.

At this time, the corresponding class will generally be instantiated into the corresponding object, and then relevant functions and operations will be implemented through the corresponding object.

In Python, the format for instantiating a class as an object is as follows:

Object {Enter the name here} = Class Name (You can enter your parameters here)

As you can see, if you want to instantiate the class, you just need to add parentheses after the class name.

For example, the class man defined above can be instantiated as a vehicle's object by the following code:

class man:

⬜pass

vehicle=man()

As you can see, when instantiating, you only need to follow the corresponding format described above.

Run the above program, and then make the following debugging input:

>>> print（vehicle）

This is an object

#"A36FA90"

It can be found that when vehicle is output, the result is "...object...", where object means vehicle is initiated, while "A36FA90" in the above output result is the specific storage space of vehicle.

It is worth noting that there may be multiple objects under the same class, that is, multiple different objects can be instantiated based on one class. Several different objects may have some common features and functions, but they represent different individuals. For example, under the human class, not only the object vehicle can be instantiated, but also car and bus can be instantiated.

Although vehicle, car, and bus have some common features or methods, such as having the function of eating and having the characteristics of hair, body, etc. (because they are instantiated based on the same class), these objects represent different individuals and are different. Modifying the object vehicle will not affect other objects such as car and bus.

We might as well follow the program running above and enter the following code for demonstration:

> > create this object

> > vehicle = man ()

> > create this object

> > car = man ()

> > view information about these objects

⍰>>> print(car)

>>>> print(vehicle)

Therefore, the two objects belong to different individuals, and communication between the two objects is possible, but there is no inevitable influence.

With this, we have completed a brief introduction to classes in Python.

In the next chapter, we will in detail discuss about loops. Follow along!

Chapter 14: How to create Loops in python?

Machine learning often relies on repeating a task until it becomes a perfect sample for the query. To significantly achieve these results in Python we need to effectively use Loops. Python offers a variety of loop structures in their libraries.

In this chapter, we will in detail discuss various loops using examples.

Let us do it!

What is a Loop?

To say in simple words Loop is a programming structure that can repeat a task as many times you need. You can control the number of times a structure can loop using different logical evaluations.

In this chapter, we will in detail discuss for and while loop with examples.

Before discussing in detail about Loops we suggest you understand the concept of Judgement in control flow statements adequately. Judgment is a layman concept that processes the logical entity only when the conditions are met.

If the conditions are not met then the program either stops or destroys by itself.

In real life example, we can use traffic lights to help you understand this fundamental concept that is necessary to understand looping structures.

You can't cross the road when a red light is shown because it is the condition that needs to be followed. Judgment is also essentially used in conditional and case statements.

However, in this chapter, we will only discuss looping structures.

Follow along!

while statement

The while statement in Python is mainly used to control the repeated execution of a statement.

The basic usage format of the while statement is as follows:

While (Enter the logical value)

{

   Enter the statements;

}

Among them, the else clause part can be omitted if it is not needed.

How to use While statement?

The while statement is very convenient to use. For example, you want to repeatedly output "I like This programming language!". Such contents can be realized through the following procedures.

 instance=True

☐ while instance:

☐ print("I like This programming language!")

Of course, this program is a dead-loop program. The so-called dead loop means that the loop will not terminate but will continue to run.

This kind of dead loop program is generally not recommended and is only used for demonstration here.

As can be seen, after executing the program, the following contents will be repeatedly shown as an output:

I like This programming language!

I like This programming language!

I like This programming language!

I like This programming language!

...

At this point, the reader has learned to write a simple while loop statement without an else clause.

Here is another statement, that explains about while loop using an else clause:

instance=False

⬚while instance:

⬚print("I like this programming language")

else:

print ("This is not a good language")

In this program, because the condition is false, it will enter the else clause to partially execute the corresponding contents, and the output result of the program will be :

This is not a good language

In Python, you can use an if statement under a while statement or you can use a while statement under an if statement. This way of using the current statement or other statements under a certain statement is called nested use.

For example, if you want a program to cycle 10 times, outputting "even" for the first 5 times and "odd" for the last 5 times, you can write as follows:

first=0

⬚while first<10:

if first<5:

⬚print("even")

⬚else:

print("odd")

first=first+1

At this time, the if statement is below the while statement. The if statement mainly determines whether it is the first 5 outputs or the last 5 outputs, and the variable A is mainly used to control the number of cycles.

The output of the current program is:

even

☐even

even

even

even

☐odd

☐odd

odd

odd

odd

It can be seen that the required functions have been successfully implemented.

In the next section, we will in detail discuss for loop.

Follow along!

⌞OBJ⌟for loop

The for statement in Python is another kind of loop statement and is used very much.

For statements are executed in the following format:

For in collection: execute this section

It can be seen that the for statement in Python is mainly implemented by traversing the elements in the set in turn. The set in question is not a data type of set, but an object composed of multiple elements, which can be a list, a file object, or some other object with multiple elements.

How to use for loop?

If you need to output all the elements in a list, in turn, you can easily use the for loop.

For example, you need to output the following elements of the list

list =["Python", "Java", "Internet ", " Deep learning", "Hadoop"] in sequence, which can be implemented by the following code:

list =["Python","Java","Internet","Deep Learning","Hadoop "]

for instance

list: print (instance)

In this code, the list is defined first, and then each element in the list is iterated through the for statement loop in turn. The instance in the program is equivalent to a variable, and the element taken by the current loop in the list can be obtained every time the variable is iterated.

The instance is just a variable name and can be replaced by other names, such as entity, result, etc.

The results of this program are as follows:

Python Java Internet Deep learning Hadoop

⬚As you can see, each element in the list has been successfully removed in turn.

For statements are often used with the range () function. the range(a,b) function can generate a series of serial data from the number a to the number b, so it can control the number of cycles and the value of i during the cycle.

For example, if you want to output numbers 1 to 20, you can do this by the following procedure:

for extra in range(0,20):

⬚print(extra+1)

In this program, 0 ~ 19 is generated through range(0,20), and the variable extra will be added with 1 each time. Since the value of extra in this cycle is 0 ~ 19 and the data to be output is 1 ~ 20, it is only necessary to directly output extra+1 at the time of output.

It can be seen that the data generated by the range () function are generated in sequence. if the interval between the data to be generated is not 1, but 3, 5, -1 and other numbers, only the step size of the range () needs to be set. In general, the step size is specified in the third parameter of range ().

For example, you can enter the following program:

for example in range(1,10,3):

▢print(example)

The output at this time is:

1

▢4

7

It can be seen that the interval between the data is the set step size of 3.

Next, let's look at a for statement with nesting.

For example, if it is necessary to sequentially determine whether each number from 1 to 10 is an even number or an odd number and output the determination result, it can be realized by the following procedure:

For instance in range (1,11):

if instance% 2 = = 0:

print (str (instance)+"even")

else:

print (str (instance)+"odd")

The program judges whether this number can be divisible by 2 through the remainder operation.

If it can be divisible, it means that the number is even, otherwise, it is odd.It can be seen that relevant functions can already be realized by the output shown.

⸨OBJ⸩ Interrupt Mechanism

In the process of program execution, for example, in the loop structure, when it is desired to satisfy a certain condition or the program is executed to a certain place, the loop or the program is allowed to interrupt execution, that is, the program behind the loop body or the program behind the corresponding program block is not executed, and the corresponding function can be realized by using the interrupt mechanism of program execution.

Generally speaking, the interrupt mechanism is often used in the loop body to better realize the withdrawal and use of the loop.

The interrupt mechanism in the loop body is generally divided into two structures: break statement structure and continue statement structure.

The application situations of these two kinds of interrupt statements are different, which will be introduced separately.

Break statement

The break statement can force the loop execution to stop. A break statement is used in a loop statement. If a break occurs, the execution of the loop will be stopped directly.

The function of a break statement, like its name, is to break the execution of a program. Break statements are often used in loop structures. When a break statement appears in the loop structure, the loop can be forced to stop and then exit the loop.

1. break statement is used in while loop

If a break statement appears in the while loop, it will exit the while loop and continue to execute the following.

For example, if you want to use the while loop to output numbers 1 to 9 in sequence, you can write as follows:

first=1

while first:

☐print(first)

☐first=first+1

☐if first==10:

☐break

It can be seen that if there is no if statement in the above program, the program will be executed forever and will not stop, i.e. a dead loop will occur. Add an if statement, and then use a break statement in the if statement, which means that if the conditions in the if statement is met, the break statement is executed, and after the break statement is executed, the while loop is exited.

In the above program, A will add 1 to each cycle. When A adds 10 to the value, the output at the top is just 9, that is to say, there is no need to recycle next time and the execution of the cycle can be exited.

2. break statement is used in for loop

In addition to breaking in the while loop, you can also break in the for loop.

In the for loop, you can easily output numbers 5 to 8 using the following statement.

For i in Range (5,9): Print (i)

If you want to output numbers 5 to 7 without changing the above program, you can add the following break statement for interrupt control:

for first in range(5,9):

⏹print(first)

⏹if first>6:

⏹break

In the above program, when i in the loop is executed to 7, the execution of the loop needs to be interrupted after outputting 7, so whether the current I is executed to 7 is judged by if i>6. If this condition is met, I have already reached 7 at this time, and the loop can be interrupted by a break statement.

The final output of the above program is as follows:

5

⏹6

⏹7

continue statement

The continue statement is another interrupt structure statement, whose function is to force the execution of this time in the loop to stop and jump directly to the next execution, which is different from the function of the break statement.

The continue statement is the statement placed in the loop statement to end the loop. First of all, we should know that the loop is divided into many times, and the continue statement terminates the loop, not the loop.

In the same way, let's give you some examples of the application of continue statements.

Here is an example:

if(i==22)

```
print( Enter the statements)
```

```
continue:
```

In the above example, the statement will be executed only when the condition is met. If the condition is not met it will continue to proceed with the other statements that are present.

With this, we have completed a brief introduction to loops in this chapter. I hope you had a good time learning different concepts related to Python in this book.

Now it is your time to create your projects and improve your programming abilities.

All the best!

Conclusion

Glad that you have reached the end of this book.

I hope you have enjoyed the content provided in the book as much we loved making this book.

What to do next?

As you have completed a complex and thorough book that deals with Python programming it is now a huge test for you to apply your programming skills on real time projects. There are a lot of open-source projects that are waiting for a contribution. Remember that reading a lot of Python code will also help you understand the programming logics that python possesses.

That's it! Thanks for purchasing this book again and All the best!

www.ingramcontent.com/pod-product-compliance
Lightning Source LLC
Chambersburg PA
CBHW071106050326
40690CB00008B/1135